The Canterbury Tales

LONGMANS, GREEN AND CO.
55 FIFTH AVENUE, NEW YORK
221 EAST 20TH STREET, CHICAGO
TREMONT TEMPLE, BOSTON
128 UNIVERSITY AVENUE, TORONTO

LONGMANS, GREEN AND CO. LTD.
39 PATERNOSTER ROW, E C 4, LONDON
53 NICOL ROAD, BOMBAY
6 OLD COURT HOUSE STREET, CALCUTTA
167 MOUNT ROAD, MADRAS

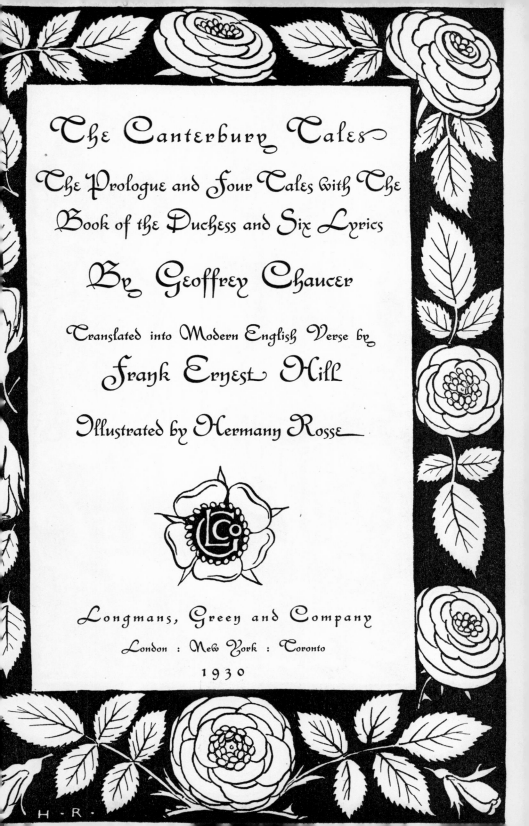

The Canterbury Tales

The Prologue and Four Tales with The Book of the Duchess and Six Lyrics

By Geoffrey Chaucer

Translated into Modern English Verse by

Frank Ernest Hill

Illustrated by Hermany Rosse

Longmans, Green and Company

London : New York : Toronto

1930

HILL

CHAUCER'S CANTERBURY TALES

First Edition May 1930
Reprinted August 1930

TO MY MOTHER
FLORENCE WATKINS HILL

ACKNOWLEDGMENTS

BESIDES the help which has been available because of the work of Chaucerian scholars and earlier translators, I have received assistance from the following: my wife, Elsa Hempl Hill, who has encouraged and aided me more than I can say; my son Russell, whose translation of lines 1610–1614 of The Knight's Tale I have used; Joseph Auslander, Prof. C. K. Chase, Cleveland B. Chase, John W. Chase, Percy MacKaye, Sister Monica of the Brown County Ursulines, and Prof. John P. Tatlock. I appreciate especially the cordial assistance of Mr. MacKaye and Prof. Tatlock who, though themselves the authors of the fine prose translation of Chaucer, have been most cordial toward this attempt in verse. I must also testify here to the help of two Chaucer-lovers who are no longer living: Ewald Flügel, with whom I first studied Chaucer and whose irresistible enthusiasm is still a living thing to me, and Raymond MacDonald Alden, who first encouraged me to make a translation into modern English verse.

The translation in which Dr. Alden was interested, that of The Pardoner's Tale, appeared in "Poems of the English Race," edited by Raymond MacDonald Alden, copyright, 1921, by Charles Scribner's Sons. This version was greatly altered for use in "The Winged Horse Anthology," edited by Joseph Auslander and Frank Ernest Hill, copyright, 1929, by Doubleday, Doran & Company. The poem as it appears in the present volume is again greatly changed, but is used with the permission of both the foregoing publishers.

I wish to thank Messrs. Doubleday, Doran & Co. for permission to reprint "The Complaint of Chaucer to His Empty Purse" from "The Winged Horse" by Joseph Auslander and Frank Ernest Hill, copyright, 1927, by Doubleday, Doran & Co.; and a portion of "The Book of the Duchess" from "The Winged Horse Anthology" by Joseph Auslander and Frank Ernest Hill, copyright, 1929, by Doubleday, Doran & Co.

"The Book of the Duchess" as here presented is a shortened version of the original. For typographical reasons I have not indicated where omissions occur, and needless to say, should the reception of this volume, which I regard as something of an experiment, seem to warrant my doing further work with Chaucer, I shall eventually offer the poem in its complete and perhaps less readable form. The other texts are given in full from the point where they begin—the prologues of the various tales have not been used.

F.E.H.

The Wife of Bath

Contents

The Unknown Poet

I

ALTHOUGH Geoffrey Chaucer is the most friendly of all the great poets of the world, he is the least known.

I do not mean that he lacks reputation: his reputation is justly great. I do not mean that his readers have been few: those who have read a little of him are legion. Yet to accept golden opinions about a poet, or to get a slight acquaintance with him is not knowledge. Either is far from that brooding familiarity with phrase and feeling which many of us have for poets like Keats, Wordsworth, or Whitman. And few have this for Chaucer, though many have sought it. Despite an infinite charm and humanity he is, in proportion to his importance, the most legendary of poets.

This should be regarded as a fact, not as a reproach. An English poet, Chaucer wrote in a different English from what we know. He himself brought his language to literary flower, and though it shaped the character of our later speech and writing, for purposes of literature it may be said to have died with him. In order to possess him, we must learn it almost as though it were a foreign language. And Chaucer's peculiar misfortune (and ours) is that Middle English, while actually so different from Modern English, seems fairly close to it.   We assume it can be mastered with a casual amount of study, and though it never is, the illusion of ease persists.   Convinced that Chaucer is too English to approach as a foreign poet, we are not honest enough to admit that he is generally but half-appreciated as a native one—that, though greater than Browning, Tennyson, Byron, Wordsworth, or Spenser, he is less read on the whole than Macaulay, Longfellow, or Goldsmith.

II

A poet in a lost language can be reached by going to him in his own speech, or by translating him into ours.   With the great foreign poets we have followed both methods.   I should like to believe that in Chaucer's case the first would be sufficient.   Yet for many years every conceivable incentive to discovering him in Middle English has been in operation, and there is no reason to hope for more Chaucer readers in the future than we have had in the past.   The truth is that the number of people who will master a dead language for the purpose of knowing one great poet is never likely to be large, and in Chaucer's case many have saluted him but few have learned to read him well.

On the other hand, Chaucer has suffered, as compared with poets like Homer and Virgil, from the lack of adequate translations.   Should we put him in the same position as these foreign poets, we might end by getting a far wider and a considerably closer enjoyment of him.

The idea of translating Chaucer into our own English is not new.   It came to Dryden two hundred and fifty years ago.   It came at a later date to Wordsworth, to poets like Percy MacKaye and to distinguished Chaucer scholars like

Skeat and Professor Tatlock. Indeed, Dryden's "Palamon and Arcite," a rendering of The Knight's Tale, and his translation of The Nun's Priest's Tale, were widely read for a hundred and fifty years. They were both included by Lipscomb in 1795 in a complete translation of "The Canterbury Tales," done by ten authors in the neo-classical fashion, and containing Pope's translation of The Merchant's Tale. Yet just as this anthology died with the already quickening romantic revival, so the other verse renderings of Chaucer have either been fragmentary like Wordsworth's, or, like the ten tales done by Professor Skeat, have failed to establish themselves. Such failure has perhaps been partly due to the peculiar difficulties of translating from a language paradoxically both close to ours and remote from it. Again, it may go back to the tentative attitude of most of the translators: possibly Dryden alone has translated Chaucer into verse with a confidence that his work was needed and could be successfully done. At any rate, the excellent prose translation of Professor Tatlock and Mr. MacKaye is now the only version widely and actively in use. A place still remains for a Chaucer that is modern poetry.

III

In attempting this volume I have had one consideration in mind above all others: a Chaucer in modern verse, whatever its defects, at least provides accessibility. And I have felt that even with those who have read Chaucer widely (I naturally exclude Chaucerian scholars), he has too often been seen in a blurred and fragmentary fashion. There is a tendency to forget the astounding variety and richness of his genius. If we are challenged, we confess him to be the greatest of English narrative poets, yet many (and this is especially true in America) who are wide readers of modern poetry might not think of Chaucer if asked to name the three greatest narrative poems in English, or might be unable to specify some of his best tales by name. Again, we know that by general critical assent Chaucer is acknowledged to have married humor and poetry more successfully than any other English poet, yet most of us have a feeble sense of how he has done it. Few, for instance, realize that as a satirist (though satire is only an aspect of his humor) he is greater than Jonson, Pope, Dryden, or Byron. In a similar sense there is no sufficient understanding of the sheer beauty of Chaucer's verse. This may be chiefly due to difficulties of pronunciation, yet while Chaucer's charm is commonly recognized (though too generally associated with the idea of naïveté), the enjoyment of a ripe beauty in him rivalling Spenser, Keats, and Wordsworth has been limited to a small number of poetry lovers. Finally, there is in Chaucer that blend of realistic sense and sheer vitality, fusing with the other qualities I have listed, which make him one of the great spokesmen for an age; and this too is insufficiently recognized. Yet if we value Dante as the voice of the mediæval soul aflame with spiritual love and religious fervor, and Spenser as the interpreter of a ripe Renaissance already tinged with adolescent puritanism, then we must go to Chaucer for the most complete and realistic picture of the age of chivalry which exists in prose or verse. Here are written indelibly the simple beauty of the fourteenth century, now delicately tender and now boldly bright, its ruthlessness and boyish love of strife, its songful coarseness and buffoonery, its firm code of honor, its medley of accomplishment and disorder, and its consoling faith.

Perhaps what many readers have missed in Chaucer and might get more fully with the aid of a modern version, is well illustrated by The Knight's Tale.

Certainly this has not maintained a footing as one of our great English poems. It is not known as Tennyson's Idylls are known, or Arnold's "Sohrab and Rustum," or Shakespeare's "Venus and Adonis." Yet it is one of the most successful narratives ever written in English verse, and it is peculiarly notable for its sustained sparkling life, a life which persists even through full descriptive and philosophical passages. If its plot seems at times little more than a charming formality, the story achieves by turn beauty, drama and sublimity. The glory of chivalry blazes from the few lines painting Theseus marching towards Thebes. Jonson and Shakespeare must have known that singing description of the May woods as Arcite, entering them to do his lover's rites, hears them ringing with the lark and sees them shining with the new sun. And where could Spenser find a model more sensuously rich yet pertinently restrained than Chaucer as he tells about the lists where Palamon and Arcite are to fight for Emely? Here are the temples wrought of iron or alabaster, decked with fair paintings of Venus or dark portraitures of Mars, the doors of eternal adamant, the fearsome allegories of life past and future. In such passages, or in that describing the funeral rites of Arcite, Chaucer is the master of young Shakespeare and young Milton, of the Elizabethan songbirds and the sensuous Keats. No one can understand the growth of beauty in English poetry without knowing the beauty of the Knight's Tale.

Yet it is a poem of action also. Here, told with a gentle satiric malevolence, are the preposterous quarrels of the heroes, here their ferocious hand-to-hand encounter in the

May woods.   Here are the jostling throngs and ringing clash of the tournament, borrowed so generously by Walter Scott to decorate his "Ivanhoe."   Here is Arcite's moving death scene.   Beauty and drama blend into a bright energy that few poems achieve or sustain.

And in the Knight's Tale, tucked deftly into the story and a formal deference to the Church, are bitter protests against human fate that rival Fitzgerald's "Rubaiyat."

The descriptions of the temple of Mars anticipate Milton's hell and in Theseus' final speech is a brief pre-statement of Housman's "To an Athlete Dying Young," concluding with these couplets:

> *And happier should his friend be of his death*
> *When yielded up with honor goes his breath*
> *Than when with age a withered name appears*
> *And all his glory dies upon the years.*

Finally, there is Arcite's dying cry:

> *Alas, O Death, alas my Emely,*
> *Alas, the parting of our company;*
> *Alas, my heart's queen, O alas, my wife,*
> *My heart's own lady, ender of my life !*
> *What is this world ?   What asketh man to have ?*
> *Now with his love, now cold within his grave,*
> *Alone, alone, with none for company.*

Passages like these have been scanted as mere islands in a poetry too genial, satiric and realistic to achieve "high seriousness."   I prefer, with "Trouthe" in mind, and parts of the "Book of the Duchess," with the Pardoner's Tale and "Criseyde," to think of such lines as representing a strong and even supreme aspect of Chaucer, not less important because not constantly expressed.

Yet if to know the Knight's tale is to reap a richness of beauty, drama and meaning, to know the Prologue or the Nun's Priest's Tale or the Pardoner's Tale is to gather a different and at times a gayer harvest.   To specify, the Pardoner's Tale is probably the most triumphant blending of talk and poetry in English.   The conversations recapture for us the very accent and gesture of the speaker, and pass from coarseness to sublimity with an ease that makes tyros of Kipling and Masefield.   And in "The Book of the Duchess" is a record of chivalric love (a younger yet more real love than that of the Knight's Tale) which can be called nothing but exquisite.   In all these poems one discovers those supreme moments which poetry lives by, as when, after the rough idiomatic brutality of the rioters' talk in "The Pardoner's Tale," comes that sudden flow into sublimity with the old man's lament on the slowness of Death. Such passages, along with those which show a more playful, buoyant or satiric poet, are still too much the spiritual property of a select few.

IV

THE six tales and six lyrics which make up this volume seem to me to comprise the most highly distinguished of Chaucer's poems, long and short, with the exception of "Troilus and Criseyde," which is a book in itself.   I think they represent also most of Chaucer's significant moods, though some readers may find the collection short in ribaldry.

Naturally I am well aware of the difficulties in translating Chaucer. His closeness to modern English, sometimes helpful, is usually a stubborn obstacle. The music of Middle English is not the music of our language today. I have given much attention to the vowel sounds, rhythms, and singing feminine endings of Chaucer's lines, yet I know that in all these respects something has been lost. On the other hand, loss is inevitable in the transition from one tongue to another, and a translation of Chaucer into modern English must be first of all a modern English poem. I have kept this constantly in mind, and have been ready to depart from the pattern of the original wherever the making of vital modern verse seemed to demand departure. I have hoped for a marriage of the fundamentals of both—the humor, beauty, melody, truth and accent that are Chaucer's and the words and rhythm that make our living speech to-day.

FRANK ERNEST HILL

New York City, February, 1930.

The Prologue

The Prologue

WHEN April with his showers hath pierced the drought
Of March with sweetness to the very root,
And flooded every vein with liquid power
That of its strength engendereth the flower;
When Zephyr also with his fragrant breath
Hath urged to life in every holt and heath
New tender shoots of green, and the young sun
Half of his course within the Ram hath run,
And little birds are making melody
That sleep the whole night through with open eye,
For in their hearts doth Nature stir them so,
Then people long on pilgrimage to go,
And palmers to be seeking foreign strands,
To distant shrines renowned in sundry lands.
And then from every English countryside
Especially to Canterbury they ride,
There to the holy sainted martyr kneeling
That in their sickness sent them help and healing.

Now in that season it befell one day
In Southwark at the Tabard as I lay,
Ready upon my pilgrimage to start
Toward Canterbury, reverent of heart,

GEOFFREY CHAUCER

3

There came at night into that hostelry
Full nine and twenty in a company,
People of all kinds that had chanced to fall
In fellowship, and they were pilgrims all
Riding to Canterbury.   The stables there
Were ample, and the chambers large and fair,
And well was all supplied us of the best,
And by the time the sun had gone to rest
I knew them and had talked with every one,
And so in fellowship had joined them soon,
Agreeing to be up and take our way
Where I have told you, early with the day.

But none the less, while I have space and time,
Before I venture farther with my rime,
It seems to me no more than reasonable
That I should speak of each of them and tell
Their characters, as these appeared to me,
And who they were, and what was their degree,
And something likewise of their costumes write;
And I will start by telling of a knight.

The Knight

A KNIGHT there was, and that a noble man,
Who from the earliest time when he began
To ride forth, loved the way of chivalry,
Honor and faith and generosity.
Nobly he bare himself in his lord's war,
And he had ridden abroad (no man so far),
In many a Christian and a heathen land,
Well honored for his worth on every hand.
He was at Alexandria when that town

Was won, and many times had sat him down
Foremost among the knights at feast in Prussia.
In Lithuania had he fought, and Russia,
No Christian more. Well was his worth attested
In Spain when Algeciras was invested,
And at the winning of Lyeys was he,
And Sataly, and rode in Belmarie;
And in the Great See he had been at hand
When many a noble host had come to land.
Of mortal battles he had known fifteen,
And jousted for our faith at Tramessene
Thrice in the lists, and always slain his foe.
And he had been in Turkey, years ago,
Lending the prince of Palaty his sword
In war against another heathen lord;
And everywhere he went his fame was high.
And though renowned, he bore him prudently;
Meek was he in his manner as a maid.
In all his life to no man had he said
A word but what was courteous and right:
He was a very perfect noble knight.
But now to tell you what array he had —
His steeds were good, but he himself was clad
Plainly; in fustian doublet he was dressed,
Discolored where his coat of mail had pressed,
For he was lately come from his voyage,
And went at once to do his pilgrimage.

The Squire

WITH him there went a SQUIRE, that was his son, —
A lover and soldier, full of life and fun,

With locks tight-curled, as if just out of press;
His age in years was twenty, I should guess.
In stature he appeared of middle height,
And great of strength, and wondrous quick and light.
And he had gone campaigning recently
In Flanders, in Artois, and Picardy,
And in this short space bore a gallant part,
Hoping for favor in his lady's heart.
His raiment shone as if he were a mead
Broidered with flowers fresh and white and red.
Singing or fluting was he all the day;
He was as lusty as the month of May.
Short was his gown, with sleeves both long and wide,
Well could he sit a horse and fairly ride;
He could make songs, and prettily indite,
And joust and dance as well, and draw and write.
So fierce by night did love his heart assail
He slept no more than doth a nightingale.
Courteous he was, humble, willing and able,
And carved before his father at the table.

The Yeoman

He had a YEOMAN there, and none beside
In service, for it pleased him so to ride;
And he was clad in coat and hood of green.
He bore a sheaf of arrows, bright and keen,
And wings of peacock feathers edged the wood.
He kept his gear the way a yeoman should —
No shafts of his with feathers dragging low ! —
And in his hand he bare a mighty bow.
Close-cropped his head was, and his face was brown,

He knew well all the woodcraft that was known.
Gay on his arm an archer's guard he wore;
A buckler at one side and sword he bore;
Upon the other side a dagger swung,
Sharp as a spear's point, richly wrought and hung.
Saint Christopher on his breast made silver sheen.
He bore a horn; his baldric was of green;
In truth, he was a forester, I should guess.

The Prioress

ALSO there was a nun, a PRIORESS,
And she went smiling, innocent and coy;
The greatest oath she swore was by Saint Loy;
And she was known as Madame Eglentine.
Full well she sang the services divine,
Intoning through her nose right prettily,
And fair she spoke her French and fluently
After the school of Stratford-at-the-Bow;
(The French that Paris spoke she didn't know).
Well-taught she was at table; she would let
No food fall from her lips; she never wet
Her fingers deeply in the sauce; with care
She raised each morsel; well would she beware
Lest any drop upon her breast should fall;
In manners she delighted above all.
Always she wiped her upper lip so clean
That never a fleck of grease was to be seen
Within her cup when she had drunk.   When she
Reached for her food, she did it daintily.
Pleasant she was, and loved a jest as well,
And in demeanor she was amiable.

Ever to use the ways of court she tried,
And sought to keep her manner dignified,
That all folk should be reverent of her.
But, speaking of her heart and character,
Such pity had she, and such charity
That if she saw a trapp'd mouse she would cry —
If it had died, or even if it bled;
And she had little dogs to which she fed
Fine roasted meat, or milk, or dainty bread;
How would she weep if one of them were dead,
Or any one should strike it viciously:
She was all heart and sensibility!
Her face was fair in pleated wimple draped,
Her eyes were gray as glass, her nose well-shaped,
Her mouth full small and thereto soft and red,
But of a truth she had a fair forehead,
A span in breadth or I should be surprised,
For certainly she was not undersized.
Handsome her cloak, as I was well aware;
And wrought of coral round her arm she bare
A bracelet all of beads and green gauds strung,
And down from this a golden pendant hung —
A brooch on which was written a crown'd *A*
Followed by *Amor Vincit Omnia.*

The Nun   The Three Priests

ANOTHER NUN rode in her retinue,
That as her chapelaine served, and THREE PRIESTS too.

The Monk

A MONK was there, of much authority;
A hunter and a rider-out was he,

A manly man, to be an abbot able.
Full many a dainty horse he had in stable,
And when he rode ye might his bridle hear
Jingle upon the whistling wind as clear
And all as loud as sounds the chapel bell
Where this same lord was keeper of the cell.
The rules of Maurice and of Benedict,
These being ancient now, and rather strict,
This monk ignored, and let them go their ways,
And laid a course by rules of newer days.
He held that text worth less than a plucked hen
Which said that hunters were not holy men,
Or that a monk who follows not the rule
Is like a fish when it is out of pool —
That is to say, a monk out of his cloister.
Indeed, he held that text not worth an oyster;
And his opinion here was good, I say.
For why go mad with studying all day,
Poring over a book in some dark cell,
And with one's hands go laboring as well,
As Austin bids ?   How shall the world be served ?
Let Austin's work for Austin be reserved !
Therefore he hunted hard and with delight;
Greyhounds he had as swift as birds in flight;
To gallop with the hounds and hunt the hare
He made his joy, and no expense would spare.
I saw his sleeves trimmed just above the hand
With soft gray fur, the finest in the land;
And fastening his hood beneath his chin,
Wrought out of gold, he wore a curious pin —
A love-knot at the larger end there was !
His head was wholly bald and shone like glass,

As did his face, as though with ointment greased
He was full fat and sleek, this lordly priest.
His fierce bright eyes that in his head were turning
Like flames beneath a copper cauldron burning,
His supple boots, the trappings of his steed,
Showed him a prelate fine and fair indeed !
He was not pale like some tormented ghost.
He loved a fat swan best of any roast.
His palfrey was as brown as is a berry.

The Friar

THERE was a FRIAR, a wanton and a merry,
Licensed to beg — a gay, important fellow.
In all four orders no man was so mellow
With talk and dalliance. He had brought to pass
The marrying of many a buxom lass,
Paying himself the priest and the recorder:
He was a noble pillar to his order !
He was familiar too and well-beloved
By all the franklins everywhere he moved
And by good women of the town withal,
For he had special powers confessional
As he himself would let folk understand:
He had been licensed by the Pope's own hand !
Full sweetly would he listen to confession,
And very pleasantly absolved transgression;
He could give easy penance if he knew
There would be recompense in revenue;
For he that to some humble order hath given —
Is he not by that token all but shriven ?

For if he gave, then of a certain, said he,
He knew the man was penitent already!
For many a man may be so hard of heart
He may not weep, though sore may be his smart,
Therefore his case no tears and prayers requires:
Let him give silver to the needy friars!
Always he kept his tippet stuffed with knives
And pins, that he could give to comely wives.
And of a truth he had a merry note,
For he could sing and play upon the rote —
There he would take the prize for certainty.
His neck was white as is the *fleur-de-lys*.
He was as strong as any champion.
As for the inns, he knew them every one,
Their hosts and barmaids too — much better than
He'd know a leper or a beggar-man;
For it was not for such a one as he
To seek acquaintance in the company
Of loathsome lepers — no, not for a minute!
There was no decency or profit in it.
One should avoid such trash and cultivate
Vendors of food and folk of rich estate.
And if a profit was to be expected
No courtesy or service he neglected.
There was no man so able anywhere —
As beggar he was quite beyond compare.
He paid a fee to get his hunting ground;
None of his brethren dared to come around;
For though a widow might not own a shoe,
So pleasant was his *In principio*,
That he would have a farthing ere he went;

His profits more than paid him back his rent !
And like a puppy could he romp; yet he
Could work on love days with authority,
For he was not a monk threadbare of collar,
Out of some cloister, like a half-starved scholar,
But rather like a master or a pope.
Of double worsted was his semi-cope,
That rounded upwards like a moulded bell.
He lisped a little, wantonly and well,
To make his words the sweeter on his tongue.
And in his harping, after he had sung,
Deep in his head his eyes would twinkle bright,
As do the stars upon a frosty night.
Hubert this begging friar was called by name.

The Merchant

Next, all in motley garbed, a Merchant came,
With a forked beard.   High on his horse he sat,
Upon his head a Flanders beaver hat;
His boots were buckled fair and modishly.
He spoke his words with great solemnity,
Having in mind his gain in pounds and pence.
He wished the sea, regardless of expense,
Kept safe from Middleburg to Orëwell.
Cunningly could he buy French crowns, or sell,
And great sagacity in all ways showed;
No man could tell of any debt he owed,
So circumspect he was in everything,
His loans, his bargains, and his trafficking.
In truth, a worthy man withal was he,
And yet I know not what his name might be.

The Student

THERE was a STUDENT out of Oxford town,
Indentured long to logic and the gown.
Lean as a rake the horse on which he sat,
And he himself was anything but fat,
But rather wore a hollow look and sad.
Threadbare the little outer-coat he had,
For he was still to get a benefice
And thoughts of worldly office were not his.
For he would rather have beside his bed
Twenty books arrayed in black or red
Of Aristotle and his philosophy
Than robes or fiddle or jocund psaltery.
Yet though he was philosopher, his coffer
Indeed but scanty store of gold could offer,
And any he could borrow from a friend
On books and learning straightway would he spend,
And make with prayer a constant offering
For those that helped him with his studying.
He gave to study all his care and heed,
Nor ever spoke a word beyond his need,
And that was said in form, respectfully,
And brief and quick and charged with meaning high.
Harmonious with virtue was his speech,
And gladly would he learn and gladly teach.

The Lawyer

A SERJEANT OF THE LAW, wise and discreet,
There was as well, who often held his seat
In the church porch; an excellent man was he,

Prudent indeed, and great of dignity —
Or so he seemed, his speeches were so wise.
Oftimes he had been justice at assize
By patent and by full commission too.
For his renown and for the law he knew
He won good fees, and fine robes many a one.
Conveyancer to match him was there none:
All turned fee simple underneath his hand;
No work of his but what was made to stand.
No busier person could ye find than he,
Yet busier than he was he seemed to be;
He knew the judgments and the cases down
From the first day King William wore his crown;
And he could write, and pen a deed in law
So in his writing none could pick a flaw,
And every statute could he say by rote.
He wore a simple, vari-colored coat,
Girt with a fine-striped sash of silken stuff:
This, as to his array, will be enough.

The Franklin

A FRANKLIN in his company appeared;
As white as any daisy shone his beard;
Sanguine was his complexion; he loved dearly
To have his sop in wine each morning early.
Always to pleasure would his custom run,
For he was Epicurus's own son,
Who held opinion that in pleasure solely
Can man find perfect bliss and have it wholly.
Householder he, a mighty and a good;
He was Saint Julian in his neighborhood;

His bread, his ale, were always prime, and none
Had better store of vintage than his own.
Within his house was never lack of pasty
Or fish or flesh — so plenteous and tasty
It seemed the place was snowing meat and drink,
All dainty food whereof a man could think.
And with the changing seasons of the year
Ever he changed his suppers and his fare.
Many fat partridges were in his mew,
And bream in pond, and pike in plenty, too.
Woe to his cook if all his gear were not
In order, or his sauce not sharp and hot !
And in his hall the plenteous platters lay
Ready upon the table all the day.
At sessions he would play the lord and sire;
He went to parliament as knight-of-shire.
A dagger and a purse of woven silk
Hung at his girdle, white as morning milk.
As sheriff he had served, and auditor;
Nowhere was any vassal worthier.

The Haberdasher   The Carpenter
The Weaver   The Dyer   The Upholsterer

A HABERDASHER and a CARPENTER,
A WEAVER, DYER and UPHOLSTERER
Were with us too, clad all in livery
Of one illustrious great fraternity.
All fresh and shining their equipment was;
None of their dagger-sheathes was tipped with brass,

But all with silver, fashioned well and new;
So with their girdles and their pouches, too.
Each of them seemed a burgess proud, and fit
In guildhall on a dais high to sit;
And in discretion each was qualified
To be an alderman, and had beside
Income and goods sufficient for the station,
Which would have filled their wives with jubilation,
Or else for certain they had been to blame.
Full fair it is when one is called "Ma Dame,"
And at the vigils leads the company,
And has one's mantle carried royally.

The Cook

THEY brought a COOK for this occasion, who
With marrow-bones would boil their chicken stew,
With powder-marchant tart and galingale.
Well could he judge a draught of London ale.
And he could roast and seethe and broil and fry,
And brew good soup, and well could bake a pie.
But it was pity, as it seemed to me,
That he should have a sore below his knee.
His fowl-in-cream — he made that with the best !

The Shipman

THERE was a SHIPMAN hailing from the west,
From Dartmouth possibly, for aught I know.
He rode his nag as well as he knew how;
His gown of falding hung about his knee.
A dagger hanging on a slip had he,

Slung from his neck under his arm and down.
The summer heat had burned his visage brown.
He was a right good fellow; many a draught
Of wine the merry rogue had drawn and quaffed
This side of Bordeaux, the while the merchant slept.
Nice conscience was a thing he never kept.
And if he fought and had the upper hand,
By water he sent 'em home to every land.
But as to skill in reckoning the tides,
The ocean streams, the risks on divers sides;
Harbors and moons and pilotage and such —
No one from Hull to Carthage knew so much.
Bold and yet wise in what he undertook,
With many a bitter storm his beard had shook;
He knew well all the harbors as they were
From Gothland to the Cape of Finisterre,
And every creek in Brittany and Spain.
The ship he sailed was called the *Madelaine*.

The Doctor

A DOCTOR OF PHYSIC there was with us, too.
In all the world was not another who
Matched him in physic and in surgery,
For he was grounded in astrology.
Much could he help his patients with his powers,
Selecting well the most auspicious hours,
When the ascendant ruled, and he was sure
To prosper in the making of his cure.
He knew the cause of every malady,
Were it from Hot or Cold or Moist or Dry,
And where begun, and what its humor too;

THE DOCTOR

He was a perfect doctor and a true.
The cause once known, the root of his disease,
At once he gave the patient remedies.
For he would have at call apothecaries
Ready to send him drugs and lectuaries,
For each of them from the other profit won;
Their friendship was not something just begun.
The ancient Æsculapius he knew,
Haly and Rufus and Serapion, too,
Avicenna, and great Hippocrates,
Rhasis and Galen, Dioscorides,
Averroës, Damascene, and Constantine,
Bernard and Gatisden and Gilbertine.
As for his diet, moderate was he,
And never ate to superfluity,
But for digestion and for nourishment.
Upon the scriptures little time he spent.
Sky-blue and sanguine was his whole array,
Well-lined with sarcenet and taffeta;
Yet he spent little, and with providence
Had saved his fees during the pestilence.
For gold in physic is a cordial; he
Loved gold on that account especially.

The Wife of Bath

A GOOD WIFE was there from beside the city
Of Bath — a little deaf, which was a pity.
Such a great skill on making cloth she spent
That she surpassed the folk of Ypres and Ghent.
No parish wife would dream of such a thing
As going before her with an offering,

And if one did, so angry would she be
It put her wholly out of charity.
Her coverchiefs were woven close of ground,
And weighed, I lay an oath, at least ten pound
When of a Sunday they were on her head.
Her stockings were a splendid scarlet red
And tightly laced, with shoes supple and new.
Bold was her face, and fair and red of hue.
She was a worthy woman all her life;
Five times at church door had she been a wife,
Not counting other company in youth —
But this we need not mention here, in truth.
Thrice at Jerusalem this dame had been,
And many a foreign river she had seen,
And she had gone to Rome and to Boulogne,
To Saint James' in Galicia, and Cologne.
Much lore she had from wandering by the way;
Still, she was gap-toothed, I regret to say.
Upon a gentle, ambling nag she sat,
Well-wimpled, and upon her head a hat
As broad as is a buckler or a targe.
A mantle hung about her buttocks large
And on her feet a pair of pointed spurs.
No tongue was readier with a jest than hers.
Perhaps she knew love remedies, for she
Had danced the old game long and cunningly.

THE WIFE OF BATH

The Parson

THERE was a PARSON, too, that had his cure
In a small town, a good man and a poor;
But rich he was in holy thought and work.

Also he was a learned man, a clerk,
Seeking Christ's gospel faithfully to preach;
Most piously his people would he teach.
Benign and wondrous diligent was he,
And very patient in adversity —
Often had he been tried to desperation !
He would not make an excommunication
For tithes unpaid, but rather would he give —
Helping his poor parishioners to live —
From the offerings, or his own small property;
In little he would find sufficiency.
Broad was his parish, with houses far apart,
Yet come it rain or thunder he would start
Upon his rounds, in woe or sickness too,
And reach the farthest, poor or well-to-do,
Going on foot, his staff within his hand —
Example that his sheep could understand —
Namely, that first he wrought and after taught.
These words from holy gospel he had brought,
And used to add this metaphor thereto —
That if gold rust, what then shall iron do ?
For if the priest be bad, in whom we trust,
What wonder is it if a layman rust ?
And shame to him — happy the priest who heeds it —
Whose flock is clean when he is soiled who leads it !
Surely a priest should good example give,
Showing by cleanness how his sheep should live.
He would not put his benefice to hire,
Leaving his sheep entangled in the mire,
While he ran off to London, to Saint Paul's,
To take an easy berth, chanting for souls,

Or with some guild a sinecure to hold,
But stayed at home and safely kept his fold
From wolves that else had sent it wandering;
He was a shepherd and no hireling.
And virtue though he loved, and holiness,
To sinful men he was not pitiless,
Nor was he stern or haughty in his speech,
But wisely and benignly would he teach.
To tempt folk unto heaven by high endeavor
And good example was his purpose ever.
But any person who was obstinate,
Whoever he was, of high or low estate,
Him on occasion would he sharply chide;
No better priest doth anywhere reside.
He had no thirst for pomp or reverence,
Nor bore too sensitive a consciënce,
But taught Christ's and his twelve apostles' creed,
And first in living of it took the lead.

The Plowman

WITH him his brother, a simple PLOWMAN, rode,
That in his time had carted many a load
Of dung; true toiler and a good was he,
Living in peace and perfect charity.
First he loved God, with all his heart and will,
Always, and whether life went well or ill;
And next — and as himself — he loved his neighbor.
And always for the poor he loved to labor,
And he would thresh and ditch and dyke, and take
Nothing for pay, but do it for Christ's sake.

Fairly he paid his tithes when they were due,
Upon his goods and on his produce, too.
In plowman's gown he sat astride a mare.

THE PLOUGHMAN

The Miller   The Reeve

A MILLER and a REEVE were also there,

The Summoner   The Manciple   The Pardoner

A SUMMONER, MANCIPLE, and PARDONER,
And these, beside myself, made all there were.
THE MILLER, big alike of bone and muscle,
Was a stout fellow, fit for any tussle,
And proved so, winning, everywhere he went,
The prize ram in the wrestling tournament.
He was thick-shouldered, knotty, broad and tough;
There was no door but he could tear it off
Its hasps, or with his head could butt it through.
His beard was red as any fox or sow,
And broad in shape as if it were a spade,
And at his nose's very tip displayed
There sat a wart, on which a tuft of hairs
Rose like the bristles on a red sow's ears;
The nostrils underneath were black and wide.
He bore a sword and buckler at his side.
Broad gaped his mouth as some great furnace door.
He would go babbling boastfully, or roar
Coarse jests that reeked of sin and harlotries.
And he would steal and charge a buyer thrice;
He had a thumb to cheat the scales, by God!
His costume was a white coat with blue hood.

Upon the bagpipes he could blow a ditty,
And piped us out that morning from the city.

The Manciple

THERE was a MANCIPLE from an inn of court,
And many a buyer might to him resort
To mark a steward's life the way he led it.
For whether he would pay or take on credit
Always he schemed so well and carefully,
That first in stock and well prepared was he.
Now is not that a gift of God indeed,
That one unlettered man should so exceed
The wisdom of a group of learnèd men ?
For he had masters more than three times ten,
Expert in law and diligent as well,
Whereof a dozen in the house did dwell
Fit stewards for the land and revenues
Of any lord in England ye might choose,
To make him live upon the rents he had,
Debt-free with honor, if he were not mad,
Or live as plainly as he might desire;
And able to administer a shire
In all emergencies that might befall,
And yet this manciple would fool them all.

The Reeve

SLENDER and choleric the REEVE appeared;
As close as ever he could he shaved his beard;
Around his ears the hair was closely shorn,
And docked on top, the way a priest's is worn;

His legs were long and lean, with no more calf
Than ye would find upon a walking staff.
Well could he keep a garner and a bin;
There was no auditor could do him in.
And he could estimate by drought and rain
What he would get from seed, and how much grain.
The horses, swine, and cows his lord possessed,
Stock, dairy, poultry, sheep, and all the rest —
Of all such things this reeve had full control,
And made report by contract on the whole,
Because his lord had yet but twenty years.
No man there was could find him in arrears.
No bailiff, herd or hind but he could tell
Their shifts and trickeries — he knew them well;
These fellows feared him as they feared their death.
His dwelling stood full fair upon a heath;
Green trees made shadow there on all the sward.
He picked up money better than his lord,
Rich were the hidden stores he called his own.
And he could please his master with a loan
That came from what were justly his own goods,
Get thanks, and also get some coats and hoods !
In youth he had applied himself with care
To learn a trade; he was a carpenter.
This reeve upon a stallion had installed him;
He was a dapple gray and Scot he called him.
A sky-blue surcoat good of length he wore,
And by his side a rusty blade he bore;
From Norfolk came this reeve of whom I tell,
Close to a town that men call Baldeswell.
Like to a friar's his dress was tucked about,
And ever he rode the hindmost of our rout.

THE REEVE

The Summoner

THERE was a SUMMONER with us in that place,
That had a fiery red cherubic face,
With pimples, and his eyes were small and narrow;
As hot he was and lecherous as a sparrow;
Black scabby brows he had, and scraggly beard;
His was a face that all the children feared.
No brimstone, borax, mercury, ceruse,
White lead, or cream of tartar was of use,
Or any ointment that would cleanse or bite,
To rid him of his little pimples white,
Or of the knobs that sat upon his cheeks.
Garlic he loved, and onions, too, and leeks,
And wine as red as blood and wondrous strong.
Then like a madman would he shout ere long,
And when the wine within him held its sway,
Then not a word but Latin would he say.
He had some phrases, only two or three,
Such things as he had learned from some decree —
No wonder, for he heard it all the day;
Besides, ye know full well how any jay
Can cry his "Wat !" as well as the pope can.
But in some other matter probe the man,
Then he had spent all his philosophy:
And "*Questio quid juris*" would he cry !
He was a decent rascal and a kind;
A better fellow nowhere could ye find.
Let any man give him a quart of wine,
He might a twelve month have his concubine,
And never be reproached by word or eye;
And he could pluck a greenhorn on the sly.

And if he made a comrade anywhere,
Then would he teach him not to have a care
In such a case for the archdeacon's curse —
Unless, indeed, his soul were in his purse,
For in his purse his punishment should be.
"Your purse — that's the archdeacon's hell !" said he.
But here I hold it was a lie he said;
Let guilty men of curses be afraid —
They slay the soul as absolutions save it;
Also he should beware a *significavit*.
All the young girls within the diocese
The man could frighten or could leave at peace,
Their secrets knew, and was their counsellor.
A monstrous garland on his head he wore,
That might have hung upon an alehouse stake.
He had made himself a buckler of a cake.

The Pardoner

THE summoner brought a noble PARDONER
Of Roncivalles, his fellow traveller
And crony, lately from the court at Rome,
Loudly he sang, "Come hither, love, O come !"
The summoner bore him bass — a mighty voice:
Never made trumpet half so loud a noise.
This pardoner had hair yellow as wax,
But smooth it hung, as hangs a hank of flax,
And down in strings about his neck it fell
And all about his shoulders spread as well;
Yet thin in wisps it lay there, one by one.
But hood, for jollity, the man would none,

Safe in his wallet it was packed away;
He thought he kept the fashion of the day;
Hair loose, save for his cap, his head was bared.
His bulging eyeballs like a rabbit's glared.
He had a vernicle sewed on his cap.
His wallet lay before him in his lap,
Brim full of pardons piping hot from Rome.
As small as any goat's his voice would come,
Yet no beard had he nor would ever have,
But all his face shone smooth as from a shave;
I think he was a gelding or a mare.
But at his trade, from Berwick unto Ware
There was no pardoner could go his pace.
For in his bag he kept a pillow-case
That was, he said, our Blessed Lady's veil;
He claimed to own the fragment of the sail
That Peter had the time he walked the sea
And Jesu saved him in his clemency.
He had a cross of latten set with stones,
And in a glass a handful of pig's bones.
But with these relics when he had in hand
Some humble parson dwelling in the land,
In one day he could get more revenue
Than would the parson in a month or two.
And thus with tricks and artful flattery
He fooled both flock and parson thoroughly.
But let us say, to make the truth less drastic,
In church he was a fine ecclesiastic;
Well could he read a lesson or a story,
But best of all he sang an offertory;
For well he knew that when the song was sung

Then he must preach, and smoothly file his tongue
For silver, as he could full cunningly —
Therefore he sang so loud and merrily.

Now in few words I have rehearsed for you
Number, array, and rank, and told you too
Wherefore they came to make a company
In Southwark, at this noble hostelry,
The Tabard, standing close beside the Bell.
But now the time is come when I should tell
Of how we bore ourselves that night when we
Had all alighted at that hostelry;
Then shall I say what on the road befell,
And all else of our pilgrimage as well.
But first I pray that in your courtesy
Ye will not deem it my vulgarity
If I am wholly frank in my narration
Both of their manners and their conversation,
And give their words exactly as they fell;
For this I know — and ye must know as well —
That whoso tells a tale after a man
He must repeat as closely as he can
What has been said, and every word include,
Though much of what he writes be broad and rude;
Else must he make the tale he tells untrue,
Invent, or shape the words of it anew.
None may he spare, not though it be his brother,
Nor slight one word more than he does another.
For Christ himself speaks plain in holy writ;
Ye know well there is nothing base in it.
And Plato says, to any that can read,
The words must be the cousin of the deed.

Also I pray that ye will pardon me
That I have nowise set in their degree
The people in this tale, as they should stand;
My wit is scant, ye well can understand.

   Great cheer our good host made us every one,
And straightway to the supper set us down,
And choicest of his food before us placed;
Strong was the wine and goodly to our taste.
Our host, a seemly man, was fit withal
To be a marshall in a banquet hall,
For he was large, with eyes that brightly shone:
In Cheapside fairer burgess was there none.
Bold of his speech he was, wise and well-taught;
In short, in ways of manhood lacked for naught.
Also he was a gladsome, merry man,
And when the meal was ended he began
To jest and speak of mirth with other things
(When we had settled all our reckonings),
And thus he said: "Lordings, for certainty
Ye have been welcome here and heartily;
For on my word, if I shall tell no lie,
I never saw so merry a company
This year together in my house as now.
Fain would I please you did I know but how.
And now I have bethought me of a way
To give you mirth, and ye shall nothing pay.
Ye go to Canterbury — now God speed you !
With good reward the blessèd martyr heed you !
And well I know that, as ye go along
Ye shall tell tales, and turn to play and song,
For truly joy or comfort is there none
To ride along the road dumb as a stone;

And therefore I will fashion you some sport
To fill your way with pleasure of a sort.
And now if, one and all, it likes you well
To take my judgment as acceptable,
And each to do his part as I shall say,
Tomorrow, as we ride along the way,
Then by the soul of my father that is dead,
Ye shall be merry, or I will give my head !
Up with your hands now, and no more of speech !"
Agreement took us little time to reach.
We saw no reason for an argument,
But gave at once and fully our consent,
And bade him shape his verdict as he chose.
"Lordings," quoth he, "hear now what I propose,
But take it not, I pray you, in disdain;
This is the point, to speak both brief and plain:
Each one, to make your travelling go well,
Two tales upon this pilgrimage shall tell —
Going to Canterbury.   And each of you
Journeying home shall tell another two,
Of happenings that long ago befell.
And he of us that best his tales shall tell —
That is, that telleth tales which are the best
In profit and in pleasant interest,
Shall have a supper (we to pay the cost),
Here in this place, sitting beside this post,
When we are come again from Canterbury.
And with design to make you the more merry
Myself along with you will gladly ride,
All at my own expense, and be your guide.
And whoso dares my judgment to withsay
Shall pay what we may spend along the way.

And if ye grant the matter shall be so,
Tell me without more words, that I may go
And quickly shape my plans to suit your need."
And we assented, and by oath agreed
Gladly, and also prayed our host that he
Would pledge to give his service faithfully —
That he would be our governor, and hold
In mind and judge for us the tales we told,
And set a supper at a certain price,
We to be ruled in all by his device,
In things both great and small. So to a man
We gave our full agreement to his plan.
And then the wine was fetched, and every guest
Drank of it straightway, and we went to rest,
And there was nothing further of delay.

   And on the morn, with brightening of day,
Up rose our host, and busily played the cock,
And gathered us together in a flock,
And forth we rode, just barely cantering,
Until we reached St. Thomas' Watering.
And there it was our host at length drew rein,
And said, "Now Lordings, hearken me again;
Here will I call your pact to memory.
If even-song and morning-song agree,
Let us see now who first begins his tale !
As I may ever drink of wine or ale
Whoso rebels at anything I say
Shall stand for all we spend along the way.
Now draw your lots before we take us hence,
And he that draws the shortest shall commence.
Sire knight," he said, "my master and my lord,
Draw now your lot, for here ye have my word.

Come near," quoth he, "my lady prioress,
And ye, sir clerk, have done with bashfulness !
Don't study here !   Fall to now, every man !"
Then each at once to draw his lot began,
And briefly, as to how the matter went,
Whether it were by chance or accident,
The truth is this — the lot fell to the knight;
And all were blithe and there was much delight.
And now in reason he could hardly fail
According to the pact, to tell his tale,
As ye have heard — what more is there to say ?
And when this good man saw how matters lay,
As one resolved in sense and courtesy,
His compact made, to keep it cheerfully,
He said: "Since it is I begin the game,
Come, let the cut be welcome, in God's name !
Now let us ride, and hearken what I say."
And with that word we went upon our way,
And all in merry mood this knight began
To tell his tale, and thus the story ran.

The Knight's Tale

PART I

The Knight's Tale

PART I

ONCE, as old stories tell the tale to us,
There was a duke by name of Theseüs;
Of Athens he was lord and governor
And in his time was such a conqueror
That none was greater underneath the sun.
Full many a wealthy country had he won,
And by his wisdom and his chivalry
He conquered all the realm of Femeny,
Which men in time long past called Scythia,
And wedded there the queen Hippolyta,
And to his country brought her home, with all
Glory and noble pomp and festival;
And likewise her young sister Emely;
And thus with triumph and with melody
With all his host in arms and pennons blowing,
I leave this noble duke toward Athens going.
    And were the story not too long to tell
I would relate in full for you as well
How Theseus and his knighthood valiantly
Conquered by war the realm of Femeny,
And of the battle that was fought between
The Athenians and the warriors of the queen;

35

Likewise how they besieged Hippolyta,
The fair and doughty queen of Scythia;
Of feasting when their wedding day was come,
And of the storm on their arrival home;
But all these things are not for telling now;
I have, God knows, an ample field to plow
And feeble oxen.   The remainder of
The tale that I must tell will be enough;
Nor would I hinder any man of you,
But each should tell his tale as it is due,
And let us see who wins the supper then !
Now where I stopped will I begin again.

This duke whereof I mention the renown —
When he had journeyed almost to the town,
All in the height of his success and pride
He saw, as suddenly, he glanced aside,
How in the highway knelt by two and two,
Each after each, a doleful retinue
Of ladies, all in black, that made a cry
So loud with woe, so full of misery
That in this world no living creature is
Hath heard a lamentation like to this,
Nor would they cease their cry of woe and pain
Till they had seized Duke Theseus' bridle rein.

"What folk are ye that with this woeful call
At my homecoming mar our festival ?"
Quoth Theseus.   "Be ye then so envious
Of my good fame, that cry and clamor thus ?
Or who hath you insulted or offended,
And tell me if your wrong may be amended,
And why all garmented in black ye stand."

Then spoke the eldest lady of the band,

When she had swooned with face so deathly drear
That it was pity her to see and hear,
And answered, "Lord, to whom Fortune doth give
Victory, and as conqueror to live,
Nought grieveth us your glory or success,
But we beseech you, of your nobleness,
Mercy and help; have mercy on our woe
And our distress, and from your heart let flow
Some drop of pity that may on us fall !
For truly, lord, none is there of us all
But duchess once or queen she used to be.
Now we are wretches, it is plain to see,
Thanks unto Fortune and her fickle wheel
That leaveth no estate assured of weal.
And, lord, to abide your presence, certainly,
Here in the temple of the goddess Clemency
We have been waiting all the last fortnight;
Now help us, lord, since it is in thy might.

"I, that bewail and weep all wretched thus,
Was once the wife of King Capaneüs
That died at Thebes (O cursèd be that day !)
And all of us that come in this array
And make this lamentation — one and all
In Thebes we lost our husbands at the wall
When under siege that wretched city lay.
And yet old Creon now — oh welaway !
That holdeth over Thebes the mastery —
He, filled with anger and iniquity,
In wicked spite and cruel tyranny,
To do their bodies shame and infamy —
The bodies of our husbands that were slain —
Hath gathered them and heaped them up amain

And now to no entreaty will agree
That they should either burned or buried be,
But giveth them in spite to dogs for prey."
And that word spoken, with no more delay
They fell face down and cried all piteously:
"Have mercy on us, wretches that we be,
And let our sorrow sink into thy heart."
 Down from his steed this noble duke did start
All full of pity when thus he heard them speak;
It seemed to him as if his heart would break
To see such piteous grief and desolate
In them that once had been of high estate.
And he embraced and raised them up, and bade
That in his good intent they should be glad,
And swore an oath, that on his truth as knight,
So well and wholly would he use his might
On tyrant Creon their revenge to wreak,
That through the whole of Greece should people speak
Of how King Creon was by Theseus served
As one that had his death full well deserved.
And straightway then, making no more delay,
His banner he displayed and rode away
Towards Thebes, and all his host along thereto.
No nearer Athens would he ride or go,
Nor take his ease — no, not for half a day,
But on his road that night in camp he lay,
And sent his Queen Hippolyta from there
And her young sister Emely the fair
That in the town of Athens they might dwell,
And forth he rode — there is no more to tell.
 The ruddy form of Mars with spear and targe,
Wrought against white, shines on his banner large,

That all the fields are glittering where it goes;
Beside the banner his royal pennon blows,
Rich-wrought of gold wherein was worked complete
The Minotaur, that he had slain in Crete.
Thus rode this duke, thus rode this conqueror,
Leading the flower of chivalry to war,
Until at Thebes he bade his host alight
Fair in a field, where he had hope to fight.
But to speak plain and briefly of this thing,
With Creon, that was now of Thebes the king,
He fought, and slew him manly, as a knight
In open field, and put his folk to flight,
And by assault the town he won thereafter
And made a wreck of wall and beam and rafter,
And to the ladies he restored again
The bodies of their husbands that were slain
To do them obsequies, as in that day
Was custom.   But too long it were to say
What clamor made these ladies at the pyre
And what lament, when upward with the fire.
The bodies passed; what honors furthermore
Great Theseus did, the noble conqueror,
Unto these noble ladies when they went.
Briefly to tell my tale is my intent.
Now when this worthy duke, this Theseüs,
Had Creon slain, and Thebes had conquered thus,
Still in that field all night he took his rest,
Then with the country did as pleased him best.
   Ransacking in the heap of bodies dead,
To strip them of their gear from foot to head,
The pillagers worked busily and fast
After the battle and defeat were past.

And so it fell that in the heap they found,
Torn through with many a grievous bloody wound,
Two knights together lying where they fell,
Young, and their arms the same, and fashioned well;
And of these two, Arcite was called the one;
The other knight had name of Palamon.
Not quite alive, not wholly dead were they,
But by their coats-of-arms and their array
The heralds knew them, and could plainly see
That both were of the royal family
That ruled in Thebes; and were of sisters born.
The robbers from the ruck these knights have torn,
And gently thence conveyed them to the tent
Of Theseus, and he bade them both be sent
To Athens, to be kept in prison there
Forever; naught of ransom would he hear.
And this great duke, when he hath done this thing,
Homeward with all his host goes journeying,
With laurel crowned as fits a conqueror,
And liveth in honor there forevermore
A joyous life — what more is there to say ?
And in a tower, from day to woeful day
This Palamon must dwell perpetually,
And Arcite too — no gold can set them free.
    And so passed year by year and day by day,
Until it fell, upon a morn in May,
That Emely, that fairer was to see
Than on his green stalk is the bright lily,
And fresh as May with blossoms born anew,
(For with the rose's color strove her hue:
I know not which was fairer of the two)
Ere it was day, as she was wont to do,

She was arisen, and garbed to greet the light.
For May will have no sluggardry by night;
The season stirreth every noble heart,
Making the sleeper from his sleep to start,
And saith, "Arise, and thine observance do !"
This brought to Emely remembrance, too,
That she should rise and honor do to May.
Now to describe her — fresh was her array;
Her yellow hair was braided in a tress
Behind her back, a yard long, I should guess,
And in the garden, as the sun uprose,
She wandered up and down, and there she chose,
Gathering now of white and now of red,
Flowers to make a garland for her head,
And like an angel sang a heavenly song.
The mighty tower, that was so thick and strong
And for the castle was the dungeon-keep
Where these two knights were held in durance deep,
Of which I told, and more shall tell withal,
This tower was close beside the garden wall
Where wandered Emely for her delight.
Clear was the morning air, the sun was bright,
And Palamon, that woeful prisoner
After his daily custom, was astir
And by his jailor's leave, paced up and down
On high where he could see the noble town,
And all the garden, green beneath him there,
Where went this Emely, so fresh and fair,
As in her walk she wandered up and down.
This woeful prisoner — this Palamon —
He paced his chamber, walking to and fro,
And to himself complaining of his woe;

Full oft that he was born he cried, Alas !
And so by chance or accident it was
That, through the heavy window-bars that stood
Of iron wrought, and square as beams of wood,
Downward he cast his eye on Emely,
And then he started back and cried, "Ah me !"
As though the sight had stung him to the heart.
And Arcite heard the cry, that made him start
And say: "O cousin mine, what aileth thee
That art so wan and deathly pale to see ?
Who hath thee done offense ?   Why didst thou cry ?
Now for God's love take thou all patiently
Our prison; for not elsewise may it be.
Fortune hath given us this adversity;
Some wicked aspect, some unhappy station
Of Saturn doomed us so, some constellation
We never could escape, though we had sworn.
So stood the stars in heaven when we were born;
We must endure it; this is brief and plain."
    Answered this Palamon and spoke again:
"Cousin, in truth, when thou dost say this thing
Thy thought is full of vain imagining.
No prison wall it was that made me cry
But that which now hath struck me through mine eye
Down to my heart; and this will be my death !
The fairness of her form who wandereth
Within the garden yonder to and fro
Is cause of all my crying and my woe;
I know not if she maid or goddess be,
But truly Venus, as I guess, is she."
And therewithal he fell upon his knees,
Saying, "Queen Venus, if it should thee please

In yonder garden in glory to appear
For me, this sorrowful, wretched creature here,
Then help us from this prison to escape !
And if it be my destiny doth shape,
By word eternal here to make me perish
Yet pity thou our race, I pray, and cherish,
That hath been brought so low by tyranny."
And with that word did Arcite fix his eye
Where that same lady wandered to and fro.
And with the sight her beauty hurt him so
That, if this Palamon was wounded sore,
Arcite was hurt as much as he, or more.
And with a sigh he said all piteously:
"The fresh and sudden beauty slayeth me
Of her that wandereth in yonder place;
Unless I have her mercy and her grace,
That I may look upon her, anyway,
I am but dead; there is no more to say."
  When Palamon heard these words, all angrily
He looked on Arcite. "Sayest thou this," cried he,
"In earnest, or dost only speak in play ?"
  "Now earnest; by my faith !" cried Arcite. — "Nay —
God knows I have no appetite for play !"
  Then Palamon did knit his brows and say:
"It cannot be great honor unto thee
That thou prove false, or shouldst a traitor be
To me, that am thy cousin and thy brother —
Each being deeply sworn, each pledged to other,
That never, though he perish of his pain,
Yea, to the time when death divide us twain,
Neither of us in love should cross the other,
No — nor in any matter, dear my brother;

But that thou shouldst forever further me
In every thing, and I should further thee.
This was thine oath and mine as well, I know;
Thou wilt not dare deny it standeth so.
Thus doubtless art thou pledged in secret to me,
And now all falsely goest thou to undo me,
And love my lady, that I faithfully
Adore and serve, and shall until I die.
Now false Arcite, thou shalt not do this thing !
I loved her first, I told my suffering
To thee, my brother pledged in secrecy,
As I have said, to aid and further me,
And therefore art thou bound, as thou art knight,
To help me, if it lies within thy might,
Or else must thou be false; I hold this plain."
   This Arcite proudly spoke to him again,
"Thou shalt," quoth he, "rather be false than I;
Nay, thou art false, I tell thee utterly;
For *par amour* I loved her first ere thou !
What wilt thou say ?   Thou knowest not even now
Whether she goddess or a woman be !
Thine is affection, borne of sanctity,
And mine is love, for a human creature burning.
Wherefore to thee, my cousin and brother turning,
Plainly my hap in love did I discover.
Yet let us say thou wert the first to love her;
Knowst thou not well how runs the old clerk's saw,
That 'who shall give a lover any law ?'
Now by my head, love's law is greater than
Any may be devised for earthly man;
And therefore positive law and fast decree
Always are broke for love, in each degree.

A man he needs must love despite his head,
He may not flee from love though he be dead,
Come she as maid or widow, or as wife.
And more, thou art not likely, all thy life,
To stand within her grace — no more am I,
For well thou knowest thyself for certainty,
That thou and I are doomed in prison to rot
Perpetually; ransom avails us not,
We strive as did the two dogs for the bone;
They fought all day, and yet their share was none.
There came a kite, the while they strove all wroth,
And straightway bare the bone away from both.
So at the king's court let each man, I say,
Work for himself, there lies no other way.
Love if thou wilt; I love and always shall,
And truly, dear my brother, this is all.
Here in this prison the two of us must wait,
And as it cometh each one must take his fate."

Between the two long was the strife and great,
If only I had leisure to relate —
But to the sequel. It befell one day,
To tell of it as briefly as I may,
A worthy duke, by name Perotheüs,
That had been comrade to Duke Theseüs
Since both were children in a fargone day,
Came to his comrade for a little stay,
To play about, as was his wont to do;
For in this world he loved no other so,
And him did Theseus love as tenderly;
So well they loved, as olden books agree,
That when one died, it is the truth to tell,
His friend went forth and sought him down in hell;

But of this tale I care not now to write.
This Duke Perotheüs loved Lord Arcite,
(Knowing him well in Thebes from year to year)
And he persuaded Theseüs to hear
His prayer for Arcite, so that finally
Theseüs without a ransom set him free
From prison, anywhere to go or dwell
But in this manner only, as I tell.

In brief, the covenant was ordered thus
Betwixt Lord Arcite and Duke Theseüs:
If it befell that they should find Arcite
Ever again, either by day or night,
In any country of this Theseüs,
And he were caught, it was accorded thus —
That by the stroke of sword his head should fall;
No other remedy he had at all
But took his leave, and homeward went with speed;
His neck is under pledge; let him take heed !

How great a sorrow suffereth Arcite now !
He feels Death cleave his very heart in two !
He weepeth, waileth, cryeth piteously;
Waiteth to slay himself in secrecy.
"Alas ! the day that I was born !" he wails,
"Now have I got the worser of two jails !
Now am I doomed eternally to dwell
Not in a purgatory, but in hell !
Alas, that ever I knew Perotheus,
For elsewise had I dwelt with Theseüs
Chained in his prison for evermore, and so
Had I a home in bliss, and not in woe !
Only the sight of her, the lady I serve
Though never in truth I may her grace deserve,

That would have been sufficient unto me !
O dear my cousin Palamon," quoth he,
"Thine is the victory from this event !
Thou mayst in prison stay and be content !
In prison ?   Truly, no — in paradise !
O well hath Fortune turned for thee the dice !
Thou hast the sight of her, while I'm denied her.
For it is possible, since thou'rt beside her,
And art a knight, well-born and bearing thee well,
That by some hap, since Fate is changeable,
Some time to thy desire thou mayst attain.
But I, that am an exile, and in vain
Seek for her grace, and so am in despair,
That naught of earth or fire or water or air,
Or any creature that created is
Can work me any help or joy in this —
Well should I die of sorrow and distress !
Farewell my life, my joy, my happiness !
    "Alas, why go folk always to importune
The providence of God, or else of fortune,
That often gives to them in some disguise
Better than for themselves they could devise ?
In one man lust for riches ever gnaws
That of disease or murder is the cause;
Another man from prison would be free;
At home by his own servants slain is he.
Infinite evils in such ways appear;
We know not what it is we pray for here !
We go like one as drunk as is a mouse;
A drunken man knows well he has a house,
But knoweth not the way to his abode;
And for a drunk man slippery is the road.

And truly, in this world so prosper we;
Eager and hard we hunt felicity,
Yet oftimes, of a truth, we run awry.
Thus all may say, and more than others, I,
Who had supposed, and great hope always shaped,
That when I once from prison had escaped,
Mine should be joy and perfect peace — no less;
Now am I exiled from my happiness !
Since that I may not see you, Emely,
I am but dead; there is no help for me."
     And on the other hand, when Palamon
Knew that his cousin Arcita was gone,
The mighty tower shook to its firm foundation
With grief and clamor of his lamentation.
And on his mighty shins each iron fetter
Shone with the tears he shed, all salt and bitter.
"Alas," quoth he, "Arcita, cousin mine,
Of all our strife, God knows, the fruit is thine !
Thou walkest now in Thebes, and thou art free;
Small heed thou hast for woe of mine, or me;
And manful since thou art, and also wise,
So mayst thou call on all our kin to rise,
And when in war thou hast this town attacked
Fiercely, thou mayst by accident or pact
Secure her for thy lady and thy wife
For whom I long in vain, and lose my life !
For plainly this is possibility:
Since thou art all at large, of prison free,
And a lord, thou hast advantage more than I
That here within a wretched cage must die.
For I must weep and wail the while I live
With all the woe that chains and dungeon give

And with the hurt love giveth me as well,
That makes of pain and woe a double hell."
With that the fire of jealousy upblazed
Within his breast, and gripped his heart and crazed
Him so with madness that he seemed to be
Like ashes dead and cold, or dim box-tree.
And then he cried, "O cruel gods who gird
This world with law of your eternal word,
And write upon a table of adamant
Your judgment, and your everlasting grant —
Of man what higher notion do you hold
Than of the sheep that croucheth in the fold?
For man is slain like any other beast,
And dwells in prison, and is in arrest;
Sickness he hath and heavy punishment
Though, God knows, often he is innocent.

"What justice lies in such prescïence
That still tormenteth guiltless innocence?
And yet by this my pain the greater grows —
That man is bound by the respect he owes,
For the sake of God, ever to curb his will,
Whereas a beast may every lust fulfill.
And when a beast is dead his pain is ended,
But man's with tears and torment is extended,
Though in this world he suffer care and woe;
No doubt there is but that it standeth so.
Be this for holy doctors to explain;
But well I know this world is full of pain.
Alas! a serpent or a thief I see,
That worketh many a true man villainy,
Go all at large, and freely choose his way,
But I by Saturn's will in prison stay;

Also through Juno's jealousy and wrath
That well nigh all the blood destroyèd hath
Of Thebes, whose walls so wide and wasted stand;
And Venus slay'th me on the other hand,
With jealousy, and fear of him — Arcite!"
    And now no more of Palamon I write,
But let him quietly in prison dwell,
And more again of Arcite will I tell.
    The summer passeth, and the nights grow long
And doubly do augment the sorrows strong
Both of the lover and the prisoner;
I know not which should be the unhappier.
For, in a word, this Palamon must be
Unto his prison damned perpetually,
In chains and cruel fetters to be dead;
And Arcite, under threat to lose his head,
Is exiled from the land he longeth for,
And he shall see his lady never more.
    Now will I ask you lovers, every one,
Who hath the worse, Arcite or Palamon?
The one may see his lady day by day,
But chained in prison must forever stay;
To ride or go the other one is free,
But nevermore his lady shall he see.
Now riddle it as likes you, ye that can,
For I will go ahead as I began.

The Knight's Tale

PART II

PART II

W<small>HEN</small> Arcite unto Thebes was come again
Full oft he drooped, and cried "Alas!" for pain,
For never more his lady should he see;
And making of his woe short summary —
Such grief no creature ever knew, for sure,
That lives, or shall live, while the world endure.
His sleep, his food, his drink he shunned, and grew
Dry as an arrow shaft, and lean thereto;
Hollow his eyes and gruesome to behold,
Sallow his hue as ashes pale and cold,
And solitary he was, and ever alone,
And wailing all the night, making his moan,
And if he heard a song or instrument,
Then would he weep; none might his tears prevent,
So feeble were his spirits and so low,
And altered so that nobody could know
His discourse or his voice though they should hear it.
And in his changeability of spirit
He showed, indeed, the lover's malady
Less than a mania which seemed to be
Of melancholy humors born, that lie
Forward, within the cell of phantasy.
In short, the habits and the mind were blown
About, and wholly tumbled upside down

53

Within this woeful lover, Dan Arcite.
　But why forever of his woe indite ?
When he had suffered for a year or two
This cruel torment and this pain and woe
At Thebes, in his own country, as I say,
One night it happened, as in sleep he lay,
He dreamed the shape of wingèd Mercury
Before him stood, and bade him merry be.
His staff of sleep within his hand he bare,
A hat he had upon his shining hair,
And wore such dress as he had worn that day
When watchful Argus trapped in slumber lay;
And said to him: "To Athens shalt thou go;
There shalt thou find an ending of thy woe."
And with that word Arcite awoke and rose.
"However great," he cried, "may be my woes,
Yet unto Athens will I go again !
Not for the fear of death will I refrain
From seeing her I love and serve, for I
Care not if in her presence I shall die !"
　And taking up a mirror with this word
He saw how grief had changed his hue and blurred
His visage till it seemed another kind.
And suddenly it ran within his mind
That, since his face was all disfigured so
With malady so long endured, and woe,
Well might he hope, if humble dress he wore,
Unknown to live in Athens evermore
And see his lady almost day by day.
And straightway then he altered his array,
And like a laborer that looked for hire,
And all alone save for one faithful squire

That both his secret and his station knew,
And wore like him a humble garb, he drew
At once to Athens by the nearest way;
And to the court he came upon a day,
And at the gate he stood and work demanded —
To drudge and draw — or what should be commanded.
And briefly of this matter now to tell,
In office with a chamberlain he fell,
One that was waiting there on Emely
(For wise this Arcite was, and quick to see
Which servants of the many served with her);
And water fetched, and was their wood-hewer,
For he was young those days and big of bone,
Mighty, and fit to see that all was done
Which any person there might bid him do.
And he had service for a year or two,
Page of the chamber of Emely the bright;
His name was "Philostratë," said Arcite.
Not half so well beloved a man as he
Ever was at the place, of his degree;
So noble his behavior was, report
Of his good name was heard throughout the court.
They said that it would be a charity
If Theseus would ennoble his degree,
And higher services for him devise
Where he might give his talents exercise;
And thus in little while his name had sprung,
Both from his deeds and courtesy of tongue,
That Theseus took him near himself, and made him
A squire of his own bedchamber, and paid him
Gold that he might maintain his new degree.
And all this time men brought him secretly

From his own country, year by year, his rent;
But worthily and wisely this he spent
And so for wonder never gave occasion.
And three years dwelt he there in such a fashion,
And bare him so in peace and so in war
There was no man beloved by Theseus more.
And in this bliss I leave him living on,
And speak a little now of Palamon.

In dark, in dungeon strong and horrible,
This seven year had Palamon to dwell.
All wasted, with his woe and great distress,
Who feeleth double wound and heaviness
But Palamon, whom love destroyeth so
That mad from out his mind he go'th for woe?
Then also his imprisonment must be
Not for a season, but perpetually.
Who hath the power in English rhyme to sing
His martyrdom and fearful suffering?
Not I; and so I pass with little stay.

It fell that in the seventh year, in May,
The third night (say those books that, writ of old,
All of this story have more fully told),
Whether by accident or destiny,
(As, when a thing ordained is, it shall be),
That shortly after midnight Palamon,
Helped by a friend, his prison broke, and won
Beyond the city, as fast as he could flee,
For he had drugged his jailor cunningly,
Making a clarey that was mixed of wine
And subtle drugs, and Theban opium fine;
That all the night, even though men should shake him,
The man would sleep, and nothing could awake him.

And thus he fled, as fast as ever he might,
And hard the day came crowding the short night,
So of necessity he now must hide him,
And to a forest lying close beside him,
With fearful foot stealeth this Palamon.
For thus he thought: to setting of the sun
There in the forest he would hide all day,
And with the night he then would take his way
Toward Thebes, and there would make his friends unite
With him, against Duke Theseüs to fight.
And briefly, either he would lose his life,
Or else win Emely to be his wife.
This was his thought — this his intention plain.
    Now unto Arcite will I turn again,
That little guessed how danger lay around him
Till suddenly in Fortune's snare he found him.
    The busy lark, the messenger of day,
Saluteth with her song the morning gray;
And fiery Phœbus riseth up so bright
That all the orient laugheth with the light,
And with his beams in every wood he dries
The silver dewdrop on the leaf that lies.
And Arcite, that at court with Theseus is
(Among the squires the foremost place is his),
Is risen, and looks upon the merry day.
And soon, to do observance unto May,
Remembering the end of his desire,
Upon a courser, quick as darting fire,
Unto the fields hath ridden for play and sport —
About a mile or two away from court.
So to the very wood of which I told
He chanced by accident his way to hold

Thinking to make a garland with a spray
Of woodbine leaves, or else perchance of may,
And loudly to the shining sun went singing:
"May, merry May, thy leaf and blossom bringing,
Welcome be thou !   Welcome, bright budding May,
I hope to get me green to make a spray !"
And from his courser, blithe and lusty-hearted,
He leapt, and straightway through the forest started,
And on a path he wandered up and down
Where all by accident this Palamon
Crouched in the bushes, scarcely drawing breath,
For very fearful was he of his death.
That this was Arcite he in nowise knew;
Little, God knows, he would have thought it true !
But so the adage runs and has for years,
That 'fields have eyes, and every wood has ears.'
Wise man is he that holds his spirit steady —
For sudden meetings find us all unready !
Little knew Arcite of his comrade there,
That lay so close and all his speech could hear,
For in the bush he sitteth now full still.

   But when of roaming Arcite had his fill,
And all his rondel had sung lustily,
He sat and fell to brooding suddenly
As lovers do, moody with their desires,
Now in the tree tops, now among the briars,
Now up, now down, like bucket in a well.
For just as Friday, always changeable,
Now shines, now soon thereafter raineth fast,
Just so can changeful Venus overcast
The spirits of her folk; even as her day
Is changeful, so she changeth her array.

Seldom indeed is Friday like the week.
   Now Arcite into sighs began to break,
Having sung his song, and sat him down to mourn.
"Alas !" cried he, "the day that I was born !
How long, O cruel Juno, shall it be
That thou wilt wreak on Thebes thine enmity ?
Alas ! confounded is and all undone
The blood of Cadmus and of Amphion —
The royal blood of Cadmus, the first man
That builded Thebes, or first the town began,
And of the city first was crowned a king.
And I am stemmed from him, and his offspring
By true line, through the royal family.
And now so wretched and enslaved am I
That he who is my mortal enemy —
I serve him as a squire of low degree.
Yet Juno works me still a greater shame:
I dare not now acknowledge mine own name !
But I that formerly was called Arcite
Am Philostratë now, not worth a mite !
Juno, alas ! alas, thou dreadful Mars !
Thus have ye wrecked our kin with wrathful wars,
Save only me and wretched Palamon
That Theseus martyreth in dungeon-stone.
And more than this, to slay me utterly
So fierce love thrusts his dart of flame through me,
Piercing my faithful heart, with care begirt,
That death was shaped for me before my shirt !
Ye slay me with your eyes, O Emely;
Ye are the cause, the cause for which I die !
On all things else that go to make my care
I would not set the value of a tare

If something I could do to please you well !"
And with the word down in a trance he fell
And lay there long, and then rose up at last.

    This Palamon, that crouched there all aghast,
As if he felt a cold sword through him gliding,
He shook for ire; he would not stay in hiding;
And after he had heard Arcita's tale,
As he were mad, with visage dead and pale
Up from the bushes thick he leapt, and said:
"Arcite, false traitor and dishonorèd,
Now art thou caught, that lovest my lady so,
Thou who art cause of all my pain and woe,
Who art my blood, and faith unto me swore,
As I have told thee oftentimes before,
And here hast made a dupe of Theseüs,
And hast thy name all falsely altered thus;
Either I perish here, or thou shalt die !
Thou shalt not love my lady Emely;
Nay, none but I shall love her — I alone,
Who am thy mortal foe, and Palamon !
And though have I no weapon here with me,
Having from jail by fortune broken free,
This thing is sure: that either thou shalt die
Or else shalt cease to love my Emely.
Choose which thou wilt; escape me thou shalt not."

    Arcite, with heart that swelled with anger hot,
When he knew Palamon, and harked his word,
As fierce as raging lion he drew a sword,
And thus he said: "By God that sits above,
Were't not that thou art sick and mad for love
And hast no weapon also — this I know:
Not one pace from this forest shouldst thou go,

But perish shouldst thou straightway by my sword.
For I defy the surety and the word
Which thou declarest I have pledged to thee !
O fool indeed !   Know well that love is free,
And I will love her — yea, for all thy might !
But for as much as thou art worthy knight,
And seek'st by arms to make thy love prevail,
Take thou my word: tomorrow without fail
Here, to no other living person known,
As I am knight, will I return alone
And armor will I bring enough for thee —
Choose thou the best and leave the worst for me.
And meat and drink this evening will I bring
Enough for thee — and clothes for thy bedding.
And, if it be that thou my lady win,
And slay me in this forest I am in,
Thou mayst well have thy lady, as for me !"
And Palamon replied: "I grant it thee."
And thus the two have parted till the morn,
Each having word of oath to other sworn.
  O Cupid, stranger unto charity !
O king, that will no fellow have with thee !
For true it is, nor love nor tyranny
Ever will share his lordship willingly;
Arcite discovered this, and Palamon.
Arcite hath straightway ridden to the town,
And on the morn, ere yet the night had cleared
Two sets of arms in secret he prepared,
Both suitable and fit by test to show
In combat which was better of the two.
Mounted, and lone as when his mother bore him,
All of this armor carrieth he before him,

And in the wood, with time and place as set,
This Arcite and this Palamon are met.
Then straightway changed the color in each face,
Just as the huntsman in the realm of Thrace
Standing within the gap with waiting spear,
When men have roused the lion or the bear,
Hears him at length fast through the forest making,
The boughs of trees and tender branches breaking,
And thinks: "Here comes my mortal enemy:
Now without fail he must be dead, or I;
For either I must slay him at the gap,
Or he slay me, if such be my mishap — "
So went with both the changing of their hue
As soon as either one the other knew.
No salutation was there, no good-day;
With no rehearsal and no word to say
At once each went and helped to arm the other,
With friendly hand, as though he helped his brother.
And after that, with lances sharp and strong
They thrust at one another wondrous long;
And then this Palamon ye would have thought
To be a raging lion as he fought,
And like a cruel tiger was Arcite;
Like savage boars they seemed to lash and smite,
That froth like foam for maddened rage. They stood
Up to the ankle battling in their blood.
And I will leave them fighting in this way,
And something more of Theseus will I say.

    Now Destiny, that minister-at-large,
That through the world in all things doth discharge
The Providence which God hath pre-ordained —
So strong it is, that, though the world maintained

The opposite of a thing, by yea or nay,
Yet sometime shall it happen on a day
That not again within a thousand year
Shall fall; for certainly our hungers here,
Be they for war or peace or hate or love,
Wholly are governed by the Eye above.
This now I say of mighty Theseüs
That for the chase is so desirous,
And most to hunt the mighty hart in May,
So that for him in bed there dawns no day
But he is clad and ready forth to ride
With hound and horn and hunter by his side;
For in his hunting hath he such delight
That it is all his joy and appetite
Himself the slayer of the hart to be,
For after Mars Diana serveth he.

Clear was the day, as I have said ere this,
And Theseus, full of every joy and bliss,
With his Hippolyta, the lovely queen,
And Emely, all garmented in green,
Forth to the hunt went riding royally.
And to the tract of wood that lay hard by,
In which there was a hart, as he was told,
Duke Theseus soon his way direct doth hold;
And for the clearing now he sets his horse,
For thither the hart was wont to take his course,
And over a brook, as on his way he flew.
This duke will have a course at him or two,
With hounds, such as it pleased him to command.

And when he came upon the open land
And gazed beneath the sun, he was aware
At once of Palamon and Arcite there,

Like two boars fighting, blow for raging blow;
The bright swords lunged and darted to and fro
So hideously, that with their lightest stroke
It seemed as if the blow could fell an oak;
But nothing yet he knew of what they were.
This duke he smote his courser with the spur
And in a flash he broke between the two
And drew his sword at once, and shouted, "Ho !
No more, I say, on pain to lose your head !
But mighty Mars, I tell you he is dead
That strikes another stroke !   But say to me
What kind of men the two of you may be
So bold and eager to be fighting here
Without a judge or other officer,
As in a tournament all royally ?"
    Then Palamon made answer instantly
And said: "O sire, what now shall more words serve
When both of us alike our death deserve ?
Two miserables, two wretches fit for gyves
Are we, that be encumbered with our lives.
And as thou art a judge and rightful lord
Mercy nor refuge do thou us accord,
But slay me first, for holy charity;
But slay my fellow too as well as me.
Or slay him first, for little though thou know,
This is Arcite, this is thy mortal foe,
Forbid thy land on pain to lose his head,
For which he well deserveth to be dead.
For this is he that to thy gateway came
And said that Philostratë was his name.
For years he fooled thee with a false belief,
Till thou didst take him for thy squire-in-chief,

And this is he that loveth Emely,
For since the day is come when I shall die
I make my plain confession: do thou know
I am that Palamon, oppressed with woe,
That won from out thy prison wickedly.
I am thy mortal foe, and it is I
That loves so fiercely Emely the bright
That I would die at once within her sight.
Therefore for death and justice do I pray —
But slay my fellow in the self-same way,
For both of us deserve well to be slain !"
    At once this worthy duke out-spake again
And said: "This judgment needs but little session,
For your own mouth, that frameth your confession,
Hath damned you — I attest it past a doubt;
Methinks we need no rope to scourge it out;
Ye shall be dead, by mighty Mars the red !"
    At once the queen, for very womanhead,
Began to weep, and so did Emely
And all the ladies in that company.
It was great pity, so it seemed to all,
That such a misadventure should befall,
For noble men of great estate were they,
And all for love alone they fought this way;
And gazing on their wounds, red, deep and wide,
Alike the greater and the lesser cried:
"Have mercy, Lord, upon us women all !"
And on their bare knees with the word they fall,
And would have kissed his feet as there he stood,
Till softened in a little was his mood,
For quick is pity in the noble-hearted.
And though for ire at first he shook and started,

He hath considered briefly, in a word,
The offense of both, and wherefore it occurred;
And though his anger them of guilt accused,
Yet both by reason he hath soon excused,
For well he recognized that every man
Will help himself in love as best he can,
And out of prison deliver himself as well.
And also on his heart compassion fell
For the women all as one before him weeping;
And in his noble heart the thought came creeping,
And softly to himself he said, "Now fie
Upon a lord that mercy will deny,
And both in word and deed the lion be,
Alike to those that come remorsefully
And awed with fear, and to a spiteful man
That proudly holds to what he first began.
Truly that lord hath scant discerning sense
Who in such cases sees no difference,
But weighs humility and pride as one."
Thus, in a word, his anger being gone,
He looked about him with more cheerful eyes,
And pleasantly he spoke and in this wise:
    "The god of love ! Ah ! *benedicite !*
How mighty and how great a lord is he !
No obstacles may stand against his might,
And for his miracles shall men do right
To call him god: of every heart he maketh
In his own way what thing his fancy taketh.
Lo here ! This Arcite and this Palamon,
Both from my prison free, that might have gone
To Thebes, and dwelt there well and royally,
And know I am their mortal enemy,

And that their death at my discretion lies —
And yet hath love, in spite of their two eyes,
Brought both of them together here to die.
Now look ye, is not that a folly high ?
Who can a true fool be unless he love ?
Behold, for the gods' sake that sit above —
See how they bleed !   Are they not well arrayed ?
The god of love, their lord, thus hath he paid
Their wages for their service, and their fee !
Yet very wise these lovers think they be
That give love service, let what may befall !
But this is yet the finest jest of all —
That she, for whom they have this jollity,
Can give them no more thanks than she gives me;
Of this hot work she was no more aware
By God, than is a cuckoo or a hare !
Yet they must try it all, the hot and cold,
A man must be a fool, or young or old;
I know this from my own case long ago,
For in my time I was a servant, too.
And therefore, since I know the pain of love,
And how a man may feel the force thereof,
As one that oft hath struggled in his snare,
Full pardon for your trespass I declare
At asking of the queen that kneeleth here,
And Emely as well, my sister dear.
And ye shall swear at once your oaths to me
Never to work my country injury,
Nor wage a war against me, night or day,
But be my friends in everything ye may;
And so I pardon you this trespass wholly."
Then to his asking swore they fair and fully,

And for his judgment and his mercy prayed,
And grace he granted them, and thus he said:
    "To speak of royal lineage or demesne —
Though she should be a princess or a queen,
Both of you well are worthy, I confess,
To wed when it is time; yet none the less
I speak for her, my sister Emely,
For whom ye have this strife and jealousy.
Ye know yourselves, she cannot marry two
At once, though ye eternal combat do:
One of you, be he loath or be he lief,
Must go and whistle to an ivy-leaf;
That is to say, she cannot have you both,
However jealous ye may be or wroth.
And therefore this condition I decree
For you, that each shall have his destiny
As shaped for him; hear now the way it lies —
This is your plan, this is what I devise.
    "My will is this, to make a clear decision
With no discussion of it or revision;
If it shall please you, take it for the best:
That each go forth as likes him, east or west,
Free of control and all indebtedness,
And this day fifty weeks, nor more nor less,
Each of you here a hundred knights shall bring,
All armed to take the lists in everything,
Your claims on her by tournament to test;
And on my promise may ye safely rest,
Upon my truth and as I am a knight,
That unto him of you that hath the might,
That is to say, that whether he or thou
Shall with the hundred that I spoke of now

Drive from the lists or slay his adversary
To him will I give Emely to marry —
To him that Fortune giveth such fair grace.
The lists shall I have builded in this place,
And God so justly by my spirit do
As I shall be impartial judge and true.
Ye shall no other ending make for me
But one of you shall dead or taken be.
And if this seems to you to be well said,
Give your opinion and be comforted;
For this your end and your decision is."
    Who now but Palamon hath joy in this ?
Who leaps aloft for gladness but Arcite ?
Who could in speech describe, or who could write
The joy was celebrated in that place
When Theseüs hath done so fair a grace ?
Then all the people there, in their degrees,
With heart and might thanked him upon their knees,
And most, and many times, the Thebans two.
And thus with hope and blithe of heart they go,
Taking their leave, and straight for home they ride,
To Thebes, that stands with ancient walls and wide.

The Knight's Tale

PART III

Part III

I THINK that men would deem it negligence
Should I forget to tell at what expense
Duke Theseus goes about so busily
To build the lists up royally and high,
That never was such noble theatre
Seen, I dare say, in this world anywhere.
The circuit of it was a mile about,
And it was walled with stone and ditched without,
And rounded, compass-like, and gradually
Built up in tiers to sixty paces high,
So that a man set on the seat assigned him
Would hinder not the sight of one behind him.
    Eastward there stood a gate of marble white,
Westward, just such another opposite,
And, in a word, there was no other place
Like it on earth within such little space;
For there was not a workman in the land,
If he arithmetic could understand,
Geometry, or carving images,
But Theseus gave him meat and princely fees
The theatre to build and to devise.
And as a place for rite and sacrifice
Eastward he made, upon the gate above,
Honoring Venus, that is queen of love,

An altar and a little oratory;
And westward, for the memory and the glory
Of Mars, he made its very counterpart
That cost him gold enough to fill a cart !
And northward, on the ramparts turreted,
Of alabaster white and coral red,
Hath Theseus wrought a temple fair to see,
Diana and the cult of chastity
With rich and noble art to celebrate.
    But still I had forgotten to relate
What pictures and what carvings nobly made,
What shape and show and figures were displayed
For sight within these oratories three.
    First in the temple of Venus mightst thou see
Wrought on the wall, full piteous to behold,
The broken slumbers and the sighings cold,
The sacred tears, the lamentations dire,
The fiery-pointed lashes of desire
That in this life love's servants must endure;
The oaths that do their covenants insure;
Pleasure and hope, desire, foolhardiness,
Beauty and youth, riches and bawdiness;
Charms, too, and force, and loss and flattery,
Spending and diligence and jealousy
(That wore of marigolds a yellow band
And had a cuckoo sitting on her hand);
Feasts also, carols, instruments and dances,
Lust and array, and all the circumstances
Of love that I can count or ever shall,
Were painted by command upon the wall,
And more than ever I can mention here.
The mount of Citheron, in truth, was there,

Where Venus hath her dwelling principal;
Well was it shown in painting on the wall,
Its garden and its amorous excess;
Nor was forgot the porter Idleness,
Nor fair Narcissus of a time far gone,
Nor yet the folly of King Solomon,
Nor yet the mighty strength of Hercules,
Nor yet Medea's magic, nor Circe's,
Nor Turnus, with his courage fierce and bold,
Nor Crœsus, rich and wretched with his gold.
Thus neither wisdom, may ye see, nor wealth,
Nor boldness yet nor beauty, strength nor stealth,
Can hold with Venus any rivalry,
For all the world at pleasure guideth she.
So meshed were all these people in her snare
Often they cried "Alas!" in their despair.
Be one or two examples here supplied,
Though I could count a thousand more beside.

The shape of Venus, glorious to see,
Was floating naked on the open sea,
And she was covered from the navel down
With green waves; bright as any glass they shone;
A small harp in her right hand carried she,
And on her head there rested, fair to see,
A wreath of roses, fresh and good of scent;
In fluttering flight her doves about her went.
Cupid her son was standing by her there,
And two wings on his shoulders did he bear,
And he was blind, as often represented,
And bore a bow, and arrows bright and pointed.

But why should I not likewise tell you all
The portraiture was wrought upon the wall

Within the temple of mighty Mars the red?
The wall was painted every way it spread
Like to the bowels of that grisly place
Men call the mighty temple of Mars in Thrace,
Even in that region grim with frost and cold
Where Mars established hath his sovereign hold.
    First on the wall a wood was painted well,
Within whose bound nor man nor beast did dwell,
With knotted, gnarlèd, barren branches old
And stumps shorn off and hideous to behold,
Through which there ran a rumble and a sough
As though a storm would shatter every bough.
And downward from a hill, under a bent,
There stood the temple of Mars Armipotent,
Wrought all of burnished steel, of which the gate
Was ghastly to behold, and high and straight;
And from it thundered such a rage and blast
That all the doors were shaken as it passed.
The northern light in through the portals shone,
For window in that iron wall was none
Through which the smallest beam of light could slant.
The doors were of eternal adamant,
And they were clenched across and all along
With toughest iron, and to make it strong,
Each pillar that sustained the temple there
Was iron barrel-thick, and bright and fair.
    And first I saw the dark imagining
Of felony, and its encompassing;
And cruel Rage that like a coal did glow;
The pickpurse I beheld, and pale fear too;
The flatterer with the knife beneath his cloak,
The great barn burning under sable smoke,

The treason of the murdering in the bed,
And Open War, covered with wounds that bled,
Strife with a bloody knife and frowning face;
With grating noises groaned that grisly place.
The slayer of himself was also there,
His own heart's blood had matted all his hair;
The nail that pierced by night the forehead bone,
And Death himself, cold, open-mouthed, and prone.
Midway the temple darkly sat Mischance
Beside Discomfort and Sad Countenance;
Madness I saw, loud-laughing in his rage,
Outcry and Armed Complaint and fierce Outrage;
The corpse with slashed throat in the bushes lying,
A thousand slain — none of the plague were dying;
The tyrant that by force his prey secured,
The town destroyed — nothing at all endured.
I saw the fire burn up the dancing ship,
The hunter strangled in the wild bear's grip,
The sow devour the infant from the cradle,
The cook get scalded too, despite his ladle.
Naught was forgotten: all ills ye might discover:
The carter by his own cart ridden over, —
Low on the ground beneath the wheel he lay.
And likewise Mars his temple did display
Barber and butcher and the smith that beat
Swords into sharpness in the anvil heat.
And over all, painted within a tower,
Conquest I saw, that sat enthroned in power.
And higher still, and just above his head,
A sharp sword hung, suspended by a thread.
And painted was the slaying of Juliüs,
Of mighty Nero, of Antonius;

For though at this time they were still unborn,
Yet here their deaths were pictured to adorn
The grisly walls of Mars, by form and face;
For everything was painted in that place
As it is painted in the stars above —
Who shall be slain or who shall die for love.
Of these old pictures let me one recall;
Though I might wish, I could not tell them all.

   Upon a chariot, armed, with wrath that glowed
Like madness throned, great Mars's statue rode.
Above his head two stars were shaped in flame,
These in the scriptures being called by name
The one Puella, the other Rubeüs.
The mighty god of war was pictured thus:
Low at his feet a fierce wolf crouched and glowered,
With red eyes gleaming, and a man devoured;
With skilful brush the artist showed this story,
Honoring Mars and setting forth his glory.

   Now to the temple of Diana the chaste
I turn at once, and thither go with haste
That unto you I may describe it all.
Well pictured up and down was every wall
With hunting scenes and modest chastity.
I saw unfortunate Calistophe,
And how, Diana being wroth with her,
She changed her from a woman to a bear;
And later she was made the load-star; so
Her fate was painted; nothing more I know.
Her son's a star as well, as men may see.
There I saw Danae turned into a tree;
Not goddess Dian — it was not the same,
But Penneus' daughter, Danae called by name.

There Acteon was shown, changed to a deer
Because he dared on naked Dian peer;
And his own hounds, that now no longer knew him,
Leapt on him there, and tore his flesh, and slew him !
And on the wall, along a little more,
Was Atalanta hunting the wild boar,
And Meleager, and many another too,
And him for this Diana slew with woe.
And other wondrous stories might ye see,
Which now I will not bring to memory.
High on a hart I saw this goddess sitting,
And little dogs about her feet were flitting,
And underneath her feet she had a moon,
Almost at full, yet due for waning soon.
And all in gladsome green her form was clad,
And arrow case and bow in hand she had;
Downward her eyes were looking, toward the ground
Where Pluto holds his realm in darkness bound.
A wife in labor lay before her there,
And she, because the child was hard to bear,
Turned on Lucina, piteously to call —
Crying: "Help, for thou canst the best of all !"
Well could he paint to life that had it wrought;
His paints with many a florin had he bought.

Now are these lists complete, and Theseüs,
That at his great cost hath embellished thus
The lists and all the shrines of which I tell,
When it was done, he liked it wondrous well.
And now of him I stay a while to write,
And speak of Palamon and of Arcite.

The day of their return approaches now,
When each should bring, to test his cause and vow,

A hundred knights, as earlier I told.
To Athens then, his covenant to hold,
Each one his hundred knights in full hath brought,
In all ways armed for war; they lacked in naught.
And, certainly, said then full many a man,
That never, since this world of ours began,
To speak of tested knighthood truthfully,
Was there, as far as God had fashioned sea
Or land, so small yet noble a company.
For all that had a love of chivalry
And coveted an everlasting name
Had prayed for part within this knightly game,
And glad indeed was he that won a place.
And should there come tomorrow such a case
Again, ye know that every lusty knight
That hath his strength and loveth with all his might,
Were it proclaimed for England or elsewhere,
Would with full will desire to battle there,
To fight for a lady, *benedicite !*
A lusty spectacle it were to see.
   And right so came they now with Palamon;
With him went knights ariding, many a one.
And some of these in coat of mail were dressed,
With doublet, and a breastplate for the breast,
And some were armed with sets of plates full large,
And some with Prussian shield would come, or targe;
And some had cased their legs from hip to heel,
And had an ax, and some a mace of steel.
Never new fashions be but they are old !
Armed were they all, and even as I have told,
According to his preference, each one.
   There might'st thou see, coming with Palamon,

Ligurge himself, the mighty king of Thrace;
Black was his beard, of manly look his face;
The circlets of his eyes, deep in his head,
Glowed with a light between a yellow and red,
And like a griffin round him did he stare
From under brows where shaggy hung the hair.
His limbs were great, his muscles hard and strong,
His shoulders broad, his arms both large and long;
And as the custom was within his land,
High on a chair of gold he had his stand;
Of white bulls in the traces there were four.
No coat of arms over his gear he wore,
That shone with nails, yellow and bright as gold;
But a great bear's skin, shaggy, black, and old.
Combed was his flowing hair behind his back,
No raven's wing shone ever half so black;
A wreath of gold, arm-thick, of fearful weight,
Was on his head, and bore a shining freight
Of stones — fine rubies, glittering diamonds.
Around his car went leaping monstrous hounds,
Twenty and more, as big as any steer,
To hunt the lion with him, or the deer;
They followed now with muzzles closely bound,
With collars gold, and collar-rings filed round.
A hundred lords came riding in his rout;
Armed well they were, their hearts were stern and stout.

With Arcite, as ye may in stories find,
The great Emetrius, the king of Ind,
On a bay steed with trappings all steel-plated,
Covered with cloth of gold well variegated,
Came riding like the god of battle, Mars.
His armor-coat was made of cloth of Tars,

With pearls encrusted, large and round and white;
Of burnished gold his saddle, beaten bright.
A little cloak was round his shoulders spread,
Engemmed with fiery-sparkling rubies red.
Like rings upon his head curled his crisp hair,
Yellow, and glittering like sunlight fair.
High was his nose, his eyes bright citron were,
His lips full, and of sanguine character
Was his complexion, sprinkled with a few
Freckles that were a yellow-black in hue;
Like lion he his eye about him rolled;
And I would guess him twenty-five years old.
Well had his beard by now commenced to spring;
His voice was like a trumpet thundering.
Upon his head he wore of laurel bright
A garland green and goodly to the sight;
Upon his hand he bore for his delight
An eagle tame, as any lily white.
A hundred lordlings had he with him there,
All armed, save for their heads, in all their gear,
Full richly clad in many kinds of things,
For trust ye well that dukes and earls and kings
Were gathered in this noble company
For love and for the increase of chivalry.
And there on every side about this king
Went leopards and tame lions gamboling.
And in this way these lordlings, all and some,
Were on a Sunday to the city come,
At prime of day, and there they did alight.
    This Theseus then, this duke, this worthy knight,
When thus into his city he had brought them,
Lodgings for each in his degree he sought them,

And feasted them, and tendered all things to them,
And sought their ease, and courtesy to do them,
That folk were well agreed that no man's wit,
No matter what estate, could better it.
Of minstrelsy or service at the feast,
Of splendid gifts for greatest and for least,
Of Theseus' palace that in rich array is,
Of who sat first or last upon the daïs,
What ladies danced the best or were the fairest,
Or which could lightliest move or sing the clearest,
Or who could speak most feelingly of love —
What hawks were sitting on the perch above,
What dogs were lying on the floor below —
Of all this will I make no mention now;
For what came after — that seems best to me;
Now if it please you, hearken carefully —
Here comes the point.   It fell on Sunday night
That Palamon heard the lark, for though the light
Showed not as yet, nor for two hours would show,
Yet the lark sang, and Palamon sang too.
And high of mood and reverent of heart
He rose, upon his mission to depart
To Cytherea, blissful and benign:
Venus I mean, well-honored and divine.
And in her hour he walketh forth a pace
Where in the lists her temple had its place,
And down he kneeleth and with a humble cheer
And a sore heart, he said as ye shall hear.
    "Fairest of fair, O lady Venus mine,
Great Vulcan's wife, daughter of Jove divine,
Thou angel of the mount of Citheron,

For that same love which bright Adonis won,
Have pity on my tears and bitter smart
And take my humble prayer to thy heart.
Alas ! I have no language that can tell
The injuries or the torments of my hell;
My heart lacks strength my anguish to betray;
In my confusion nothing can I say.
But mercy, lady bright, that well dost know
My thought, and all the ills I undergo !
Think well on this; take pity on my pain
As certainly as I with might and main
Shall evermore thine own true servant be
And always wage a war on chastity —
Give me thine aid and this shall be my vow.
To vaunt of skill at arms I care not now,
Nor ask tomorrow to have the victory,
Nor even renown, nor glorious vanity
Of tourney-prize blown loudly up and down,
But ask for Emely to be mine own,
And that I serve thee, dying as a lover;
Do thou the manner and the way discover !
For I care not if it shall better be
To conquer them, or have them conquer me,
So that I have my lady in my arms;
For though great Mars may be the god of arms,
Yet thou hast power so great in heaven above
That if it please thee I shall have my love.
Thy sovereign shrine forever will I pay
Great honor, and wherever lies my way
I will make sacrifice, kindling bright fire.
And lady, if ye grant not my desire,
I pray thee well that with a spear tomorrow

Arcite may pierce my heart.   For naught of sorrow
Shall I feel then, when I have lost my life,
Though he should win my lady for his wife.
The sum and point of all my prayer is here:
Give me my love, thou blessèd lady dear !"
When Palamon his prayer had wholly said,
Right afterwards his sacrifice he made
Full piteously, with all formalities;
But now I take no time to tell of these.
However, at last the statue of Venus shook
And seemed to make a sign, and this he took
To mean acceptance of his prayer that day.
For though the sign forecasted a delay,
Yet well he knew that granted was his boon,
And glad of heart for home departed soon.
About the third hour after Palamon
Had to the temple of Citherea gone,
Up rose the sun, and up rose Emely,
And for Diana's temple started she.
Her maidens, whom she took, at her desire
Quickly they made and with them brought the fire,
The raiment and the incense rich with spice,
And all else needed for the sacrifice;
The customary horns of mead they bore;
For sacrifice they needed nothing more.
The shrine was fair with hangings and sweet scent
When Emely, all mild and reverent,
Her body washed with water from a well.
But how she did this rite I dare not tell
Unless I speak of it in general;
Yet pleasant would it be to hear of all;
To one well-meaning it were no transgression —

Such should be free to speak at his discretion.
Her shining hair was combed and flowing down,
And there was set upon her head a crown
Of green oak leaves that glittered bright and fair.
Two flames she kindled on the altar there,
And made her ritual, as may men behold
In Stace of Thebes, and other volumes old.
And when the fire was made, with piteous cheer
Diana she addressed, as ye may hear.

"O goddess chaste of woodland and green tree,
That hast the sight of heaven and earth and sea,
Queen of the realm of Pluto, dark and low,
Goddess of maidens, that dost always know
From year to year my heart and my desire,
Keep me from thy swift vengeance and thine ire,
Which came to Acteon so cruelly !
O sovereign goddess, queen of chastity,
Thou know'st I would be maiden all my life,
And no man's lady would I be, or wife.
Thou know'st I am a maid, still holding place
Within thy crew, and love the hunt and chase,
And to be walking in the forest wild,
And would not be a wife and be with child.
Nowise I crave the company of man.
Now help me, lady, since ye may and can,
By power of those three forms thou hast in thee;
And Palamon, that hath such love for me,
And Arcite too, that loveth me so sore,
This grace I pray thee — that no trouble more
Fall on these two, but love and amity;
And likewise turn their hearts away from me,
And let their burning love and their desire,

And all their restless torment and their fire
Be quenched, or turned toward another place;
And if it come thou wilt not do me grace,
Or if my fate should be appointed so
That I of need must one have of these two,
Then send thou him that most desireth me.
Behold, O goddess of clean chastity,
The bitter tears upon my cheeks that fall.
Since thou art maid and keeper of us all
To keep me virgin give me now thine aid
And I will serve thee while I live a maid!"
    Clear burned the fires upon the altar there
While Emely recited thus her prayer,
But suddenly she saw a wondrous sight;
For one flame sank and died, then fresh and bright
Burned up again, and soon the other one
Died in the same way and was wholly gone;
And as it died it made a whistling noise,
As when the fire a sodden brand destroys,
And beaded at the faggots' ends there stood
Many red drops that shone and dripped like blood,
At which so sore aghast was Emely
She wept aloud, for well nigh crazed was she,
And nowise knew she what it signified;
And all for fear of what she saw she cried
And wept that it was piteous to hear.
Then did Diana unto her appear,
Clad as a huntress, and her bow she bore,
And thus addressed her: "Daughter, weep no more!
Among the high gods hath it been affirmed,
By word eternal written and confirmed,
That thou shalt wedded be to one of those

That bear for thee so many cares and woes,
But unto which of them I may not say;
Farewell, for here no longer can I stay.
The fires that on my altar dim and brighten
Ere thou departest shall thee well enlighten
As to the love and fortune thou shalt face."
And with that word the arrows in her case
Began to clatter loudly and to ring,
And forth she went, and made a vanishing.
Then Emely in great astonishment:
"Alas !" she cried, "what meaneth this event ?
Dian, I put myself in thy protection,
Taking the fate that comes at thy direction."
And home she went at once the nearest way;
This is what fell; no more there is to say.

    At the next hour of Mars the god of war
Arcite arriveth at the temple door
Of fierce-browed Mars, his sacrifice to do,
With all the pagan rites that go thereto.
With high devotion and heart all piteous
To Mars his orison he sayeth thus:
    "O mighty god, that in the regions cold
Of Thrace men honor and as lord do hold,
That hast in every realm and every land
The bridles of great armies in thy hand,
And fortune send'st them as it pleaseth thee —
Accept my piteous sacrifice of me !
And if it be my youth so much deserve,
And if the strength I have be fit to serve
Thy godhead, and thy company to gain,
I pray thee have compassion on my pain
Even for that hurt and all that scorching fire

Wherein thou once didst burn in thy desire,
And all the shining beauty drew to thee
Of the young Venus, fair and fresh and free,
And in thine arms didst have her at thy will,
Though on a time, indeed, thy luck was ill
When Vulcan slyly drew his snare around thee
And thereby lying with his lady found thee.
For that same sorrow that was in thy heart
Have pity now upon my pain and smart.
Young and unskilful am I, as thou know'st,
And, as I think, with love afflicted most
Of any man that life hath ever known;
Since she for whom I sigh and weep and groan
Cares not a straw whether I sink or float,
And I shall lack her mercy, well I know't,
Until by strength in yonder tourney place
I win her. Yet without thy help and grace
My strength, I know full well, will not avail me;
Then in the fight tomorrow do not fail me,
O lord, for that same fire that burned in thee
Of old, and for the flame that scorcheth me.
Make it that I tomorrow the victor be;
Mine be the toil, take thou the fame to thee !
Thy sovereign temple honor will I pay
Above all others, and strive in every way
To give thee joy and thy strong craft to ply,
And in thy temple hang my flag on high
And all the weapons of my company;
And ever more, until the day I die,
I will make lasting fire before thee burn;
And to this vow I bind myself in turn:
My beard and hair that now are hanging long,

And never in the past have known the wrong
Of shears or razor, I to thee will give,
And thy true servant be the while I live.
Now pity, lord, pity my grievous sorrow:
Give me but this — the victory tomorrow !"
  When mighty Arcite thus his prayer had ended,
The rings that hung upon the doors suspended,
And the doors also clattered loud and fast,
Till Arcite as he listened was aghast.
And then the altar flames began to brighten,
And all the temple round about to lighten;
And from the floor breathed perfume sweet and soft.
And straightway Arcite raised his hand aloft
And incense on the fire once more he cast,
And other rites performed, and then at last
He heard the mail on Mars's statue ring,
And with that sound there came a murmuring
Low-voiced and dim, that said thus: "Victory !"
For which to Mars honor and fame gave he.
Joyful, and hoping now his bliss to win,
Arcite at once repaireth to his inn,
As glad as is a bird of the bright sun.
  And instantly such battle was begun
To keep their promises in heaven above,
Between great Venus that is queen of love,
And stern-browed Mars, of arms and war the lord,
That Jupiter sought vainly an accord
Between them.   Saturn then, the pale and cold,
That knew so many instances of old,
From long experience a way descried
By which the two were quickly satisfied.

Truly, great benefits in age appear,
For wisdom there and custom both inhere;
Though youth hath quicker legs its mind runs slower;
Saturn, to banish strife and doubt that lower,
Though to his nature this was contrary,
For all the trouble found a remedy.
    "Dear daughter Venus," Saturn said to her,
"My orbit, with its great diameter,
Holds more of power than knoweth any man;
Mine is the drowning in the ocean wan;
Mine is the prison, dark in dungeon tower;
Strangling and hanging too are in my power,
Rebellious murmurs and the churls' uprising,
Groans, and the poison-death of dark devising,
And vengeance I impose and fines as well,
What time within the lion's sign I dwell.
Mine is the wrecking, too, of high-roofed halls,
Falling of towers and tumbling down of walls
Upon the miner and the carpenter.
When Samson shook the pillars I was there
And wrought his death.   Control of sickness cold,
Dark treasons and sly strategems I hold;
My glance is father unto pestilence.
Now weep no more: I shall with diligence
Make sure that Palamon, that is thy knight,
Shall have his lady as thou saidst he might;
Though Mars shall help his knight, still there must be
Between you two a peace eventually,
Though ye be nowise of one temperament,
Which makes division thus, and discontent.
Thy grandsire I, ready to do thy will;

Cease weeping, for thy wish will I fulfill."

Now will I cease to speak of gods above —
Of Mars, and Venus, goddess-queen of love,
And tell you as directly as I can
Of the great deeds for which I first began.

The Knight's Tale

PART IV

Part IV

Great was the feast in Athens on that day,
And all the lusty blossoming of May
Put folk in such a happy countenance
That all that Monday did they joust and dance
And made for Venus high festivities.
But since with morning they must all arise
Early, in readiness to see the fight,
Unto their rest they turned them with the night.
And on the morrow, when the day began,
Clatter and noise of arms for horse and man
Sounded in all the hostelries about.
And toward the palace many a troop set out
Of lords on steeds and palfreys.   And therewith
Might ye have heard the armor-forging smith
At work on harness rich with many a fold
Of woven steel, embroidery and gold.
Hauberks and shields and trappings strangely wrought
And coats-of-arms and gold-hewn helmets caught
The light; and gay-cloaked lords went riding through
On coursers proud, and knights of retinue;

And squires were nailing spears and making right
The straps of shields, and buckling helmets tight,
And lacing thongs — in nothing were they idle;
And foaming steeds, each at his golden bridle,
Were champing proudly, and the armorers too
With file and hammer darted to and fro;
Yeomen and commoners with staves were out
Crowding as thick as they could move about,
Fife, trumpet sounded, clarion, kettle drum,
From which in battle bloody noises come;
All up and down the palace floors were thronged,
Three here, ten there, that great debate prolonged,
Questioning of these knights, these Thebans two;
And some of them said thus and some said so;
Some held the part of him with the black beard,
Some backed the bald one, others the thick-haired;
Some said he had a grim look and would fight —
"He bears an ax is twenty pound in weight."
Thus in the hall the words went busily
Long after sun began to mount the sky.

    Great Theseus, that from slumber had been stirred
By minstrelsy and all the noise he heard,
Held yet the chamber of his palace splendid
Till on his will the Theban knights attended,
Each having been with equal honors greeted.
Duke Theseüs was at a window seated,
Clothed like a god that sitteth on his throne,
And thither all the people hastened soon
To see him and high reverence to do him,
And for his will and hest to hearken to him.

    A herald on a scaffold cried a "Ho!"
Till all the noise was quieted below

Among the crowd, and when the folk were still,
For the great duke he spoke and showed his will.
   "Of his high wisdom hath our lord decreed
It were destruction and a waste indeed
That noble blood in battle should be spent
Unto the death here in this tournament.
Wherefore, to shape it that they shall not die,
His former purpose he will modify !
Therefore let no man, lest he lose his life,
A missle or a poleax or short knife
Unto the lists have sent, or thither bring;
Nor any sword for thrusting let him swing
With cutting point, nor bear it at his side.
And no man may against his fellow ride
More than one course with sharpened spear, but he
May thrust on foot at will, defensively.
And who in peril is, his foe shall take,
And slay him not, but bring him to the stake
That shall established be on either side;
Thither shall he be forced and there abide.
And if the chief of either side shall be
Taken, or smite his rival fatally,
Then shall the tourneying no longer last.
God speed you; forth, and lay on hard and fast,
With long swords and with maces fight your fill !
Go now your ways; so saith our lord his will."
   The voice of the people knocked against the sky,
So loud they shouted and with lusty cry,
"Now God save such a lord, that is so good
He will not have a useless waste of blood !"
Up go the trumpets and the melody,
And to the lists ride all the company;

In order through the mighty town they hold,
That not with serge was draped, but cloth-of-gold.
Full lordly there did noble Theseus ride,
With the two Thebans one on either side,
After them rode the queen and Emely,
And following that another company —
This one and that, by rank from first to last.
And thus through all the city streets they passed
And at the lists were entered in good time.
The day was not yet fully come to prime
When Theseüs was seated, rich and high,
With Queen Hippolyta and Emely,
And other ladies in degree about.
Now to the seats go jostling all the rout,
And westward through the gate of Mars there ride
Arcite and all the hundred of his side,
With banner red uplifted to the sun.
And at the self-same moment Palamon
To eastward under Venus' gate is seen,
With banner white, and bold of face and mien.
Though ye should search the world with might and main
Ye would not find two companies again
Opposed so evenly as these that day.
For there was none so wise that he could say
How either side advantage might profess
In age or in estate or worthiness —
It seemed they had been picked so evenly.
Now formed in splendid rank each company,
And every name was read from off a sheet,
That in their number should be no deceit;
Then clanged the gates shut, and the cry rang loud:
"Do now your devoir, princes young and proud !"

The heralds cease their pricking up and down,
Out peal the trumpets and the clarion,
No more now to be said — but east and west
In go the spears, couched resolute at rest;
In goes the spur, biting the charger's side;
Then see men who can joust and who can ride;
Then shiver spear shafts where the shield is thick;
On breast-bone now the rider feels the prick;
Up leap the lances twenty feet in height,
Out go the swords with flaming silver light.
Helmets they hew apart and hack and shred,
Out spurts the jetting blood in streams of red;
Now swing the mighty maces, bones they crush;
Now through the thickest press the riders push.
Strong steeds go stumbling now, and down goes all.
One rolleth underfoot as rolls a ball.
One on his feet thrusts with his spear, and one
Comes hurtling with his horse and bears him down;
One through the body is hurt, and him they take
Struggling in vain, and bring him to the stake;
And by the compact there he must abide;
Another lad stays on the other side.
And sometimes Theseus bids them take their ease
To drink or mend their strength, as they may please.
And often on that day these Thebans two
Together met, and wrought each other woe;
Each hath unhorsed the other twice that day.
No tiger in the vale of Galgafay
Robbed of her cub, more fierce or full of might
Leaps out against the huntsman than Arcite
On Palamon leapt with heart of jealousy;
No lion grim doth lair in Bellmarie

That, being tracked, or wild for want of food,
Pants for his prey and thirsteth for its blood
As Palamon to slay his foe Arcite.
The jealous strokes hard on their helmets bite,
Red from their sides the blood runs fearsomely.
   Yet end of every deed at length must be
And so at last, ere setting of the sun,
Strong King Emetrius this Palamon
Seized, while with Arcite he engaged afresh,
And made his sword bite deep into his flesh,
And twenty by their strength hemmed round and caught him,
And so unyielding to the stake they brought him.
And seeking there to rescue Palamon
The mighty King Ligurge is tumbled down,
And King Emetrius, for all his strength,
Is borne from out his saddle a sword's length,
Such fierce resistance Palamon doth make —
But all for naught: they bring him to the stake.
His bold, courageous heart availed him naught;
He must remain there, now that he is caught,
Alike by compact and by force.
                  Which one
Lamenteth now but woeful Palamon,
He that no more may go to join the fight ?
And now Duke Theseus, having seen this sight,
Unto the folk still striving, all and one,
He shouted: "Ho !   No more, the fight is done !
True judge and nowise partial will I be !
Arcite of Thebes receiveth Emely
That fairly by his fortune hath her won."
At once was noise among the folk begun
For joy of this, so loud and high withal

It seemed as if the very lists would fall.
What now can lovely Venus do above ?
What says she now ?   What does this queen of love ?
For wreck of her desire she weepeth so
Her tears come falling on the lists below.
"Now doubtless am I put to shame," she cried,
But, "Daughter, hold thy peace," Saturn replied;
"Mars hath his will, his knight hath all his boon,
And, by my head, thy comfort cometh soon."
     The trumpets and the clamoring minstrelsy,
The heralds, resonant with yell and cry,
Make merry noise for joy of Dan Arcite.
But pause and hear me well while I recite
The miracle that happened suddenly.
     This fierce Arcite, his helmet looseth he,
And on a courser through the roomy place
Goes pricking up and down to show his face,
And upward gazes at this Emely;
And she on him looks down with friendly eye,
For women, speaking generally, will go
Wherever Fortune may her favor show;
And Arcite saw her and was merry-hearted.
Then from the ground a hellish fury started,
At Saturn's asking there by Pluto sent,
And Arcite's horse well mad with terror went,
And leaped aside, and stumbled as he reared;
And Arcite, all surprised and unprepared,
Was thrown, and fell, and struck upon his head;
And where he fell he lay as he were dead,
His breast all shattered by his saddle-bow.
As black he looked as any coal or crow,
For all the blood had gathered in his face.

And straightway he was carried from the place
And to the palace mournfully was borne,
And quickly of his harness was he shorn,
And fair and speedily was brought to bed,
For he was yet alive and clear of head,
And always crying after Emely.

Duke Theseüs, with all his company,
Unto his city Athens now is come,
And every pomp and joy attend him home.
For he would not, despite this accident,
That everyone should feel discouragement;
It was said also, Arcite would not die,
But they would heal him of his injury.
And in another thing they took delight —
That none of them had perished in the fight,
Though wounded were they sore, and chiefly one
Upon whose breast a spear had pierced the bone.
To use on other wounds and broken arms
Some had their salves and others worked with charms,
And sage they drank, and likewise remedies
Of herbs, for they would save their limbs with these.
Therefore the noble duke, as best he can,
Comfort and honor gives to every man,
And makes a revel lasting all the night
Unto the foreign princes, as was right.
Nor shame there was, nor any discontent,
Except as at a joust or tournament,
For no dishonoring had there been at all,
Since it was chance for any man to fall,
Or by the force of twenty knights be brought
Unto the stake, unyielding though he fought.
One person all alone with many a foe,

And haled along by arm and foot and toe,
And his steed also driven along with staves,
With men afoot, yeomen as well as knaves —
Naught of disgrace could be to him in this;
No man indeed could call it cowardice !
     Wherefore Duke Theseus caused it to be cried,
Stilling all talk of bitterness and pride,
That each side stood, as much as did the other,
Victor — and each was as the other's brother,
And gave them gifts each after his degree,
And feasted them three days continuously;
And all the kings a fitting conduct showed
Out of his town a day upon their road.
And home went every man his proper way;
There was no more but "Farewell !   Have good day !"
So of this battle will I cease to write,
But speak of Palamon and of Arcite.
     The breast of Arcite swelled, the pain and sore
About his heart increasing more and more;
Despite the leeches all the clotted blood
Became corrupt and in his body stood,
That cupping failed, and bleeding from the vein,
And brew of herbs to help him from his pain.
The power expellant termed or animal,
Which cometh from the force called natural,
Could not throw off the venom, or expel,
The tubes that made his lungs began to swell,
And poison was beginning to infest
All muscles lying downward from his breast.
Nor could he help himself, in strife to live,
By vomiting or taking laxative,
For all was broken up beyond repair,

And nature had no more dominion there.
And nature having failed, give up the search
For pills and potions: bear the man to church !
All this to say that Arcite had to die —
Wherefore he bade them send for Emely
And Palamon, that was his cousin dear,
Then thus he spake, as straightway ye shall hear.
    "The woeful spirit in me cannot bring
In speech a fragment of my suffering
To you, my lady, whom I love the most;
But I bequeath the service of my ghost
To you above all other creatures, knowing
Life is in ebb, and I shall soon be going.
Alas, the woe ! the agony so strong
That I for you have suffered, and so long !
Alas, O death !   Alas, mine Emely,
Alas, the parting of our company !
Alas, my heart's queen !   O alas, my wife,
My heart's own lady, ender of my life !
What is this world ?   What asketh man to have ?
Now with his love, now cold within his grave —
Alone, alone, with none for company !
Farewell, sweet foe !   Farewell, my Emely.
Now gently take me in your arms, I pray,
For love of God, and hearken what I say.
    "I have with Palamon, my cousin here,
Had strife and rancor lasting many a year,
For love of you, and my great jealousy.
Now Jupiter make sure the way for me
To tell you of a lover well and truly,
With every circumstance considered duly —
That is to say — truth, knighthood and estate,

Honor, humility, and kinsmen great,
Wisdom, and all such things as make the whole;
As Jupiter is living in my soul,
In all this world I know indeed of none
So worthy to be loved as Palamon,
That serves you now, and will for all his life.
And if ye ever think to be a wife,
Forget not him — this noble Palamon."
And when that word was said, his speech was done,
For from his feet crept upward to his breast
The cold of death, that shut him from the rest.
And in his two arms also came at length
The loss and vanishing of vital strength.
Only the mind, the mind and nothing more,
Within his sick and failing heart upbore;
But when the heart itself was lost to death,
Then dusk fell on his eyes, then failed his breath.
Yet on his lady still he fixed his eye:
His final word was, "Mercy, Emely !"
Then changed his spirit houses, going where
I cannot tell, since I was never there.
Therefore I stop, for no diviner I,
Nor aught of souls within my book descry,
Nor those opinions would I care to tell
Of such as write of souls and where they dwell.
Arcite is cold, where Mars hath sovereignty;
Now will I speak again of Emely.

    Shrieks Emely, loud waileth Palamon,
And Theseus took his sister in a swoon
And bore her quickly from the corpse away.
What will it help to linger out the day
Telling of how she wept, both night and morrow;

For in such cases women have such sorrow,
Seeing their husbands die and from them go,
That most of them lament their losses so,
Or into such a malady are cast
That certainly they die of it at last.

Infinite were the sorrows and the tears
Of aged folk and folk of tender years
Through the whole city for this Theban's death;
Child, man, and woman for him sorroweth.
Not such a lamentation was there made
For Hector's body unto Troy conveyed,
All newly slain.   Alas, the pity there !
Gashing of cheeks and rending of the hair.
"Why wouldst thou go to Death," these women cry,
"Who haddest gold enough, and Emely ?"
No man might comfort Theseus then except
Ægeus, his old father, who had kept
Remembrance of this world, how wide in range
As he had seen it up and down with change,
Joy after woe, woe after happiness,
And told them parables and instances.

"Just as no man hath ever died," quoth he,
"Unless he lived on earth in some degree,
So never hath there lived a man," he said,
"In all this world, but sometime must be dead.
This earth is but a thoroughfare of woe
And we are pilgrims passing to and fro;
Death is the end of every worldly pain."
And more beside he said in such a vein;
And full of wisdom, with the people plead
That once again they should be comforted.

Duke Theseus now gives deep consideration

As to the most befitting situation
For Arcite's tomb, and asketh furthermore
What place would honor most the rank he bore.
And to this thought he came when he was done:
That there where first Arcite and Palamon
Had made for love their battle in the glade,
There where the trees were sweet and green with shade,
There where he had his amorous desires,
And his complaint, and scorching lover's fires,
There he would make a fire, in which they might
Accomplish fitly each funereal rite.
And Theseus then commanded men to fell
The ancient oaks, and cut them up as well,
And line them out in billets fit to burn;
And swift of foot his prompt attendants turn,
And ride at once to further his intent.
And hard upon their going Theseus sent
After a bier, and had it fully dressed
With cloth-of-gold, the richest he possessed,
And in a suit of this he clad Arcite;
But both his hands he sheathed in gloves of white,
And crowned his head with wreath of laurel green,
And laid a sword beside him, bright and keen.
And then he bared the visage on the bier,
Weeping till it was piteous to hear,
And that the folk might see it, one and all,
With day he brought the body to the hall
Where all with moaning and lament was loud.
Then clad in tear-stained black amid the crowd
This woeful Theban Palamon appeared
With ashes in his hair, and tangled beard;
And weeping most of all came Emely,

Deepest in grief of all that company.
And since he knew the funeral should be
Noble and rich for one of his degree,
Duke Theseus gave command that they should bring
Three chargers trapped in steel all glittering,
And covered with the arms of Lord Arcite.
Upon these steeds, that towered huge and white,
Were seated men; and one displayed his shield;
Another high aloft his great spear held;
The third came carrying his Turkish bow —
With burnished gold the case and fittings glow;
And at a walk all rode with mournful cheer
Toward the grove, as later ye shall hear.
And of the Greeks the noblest that were there
Arcita's bier upon their shoulders bare,
All slack of pace, with watery eyes and red,
Down the main street that through the city led,
Where all with black was hung, that wondrous high
Covered the walls and houses toward the sky.
Aged Ægeus on the right hand rode,
Duke Theseus on the left, and richly glowed
The vessels which they bore of gold all fine,
Filled full of honey, milk, and blood and wine;
Palamon too, with a great company;
And after that came woeful Emely;
The funeral fire she carried in her hand
As was the custom in that time and land.

　　Great labor went to raising of the pyre
Where should be made the service and the fire;
High into heaven itself the green top pried,
And stretched its broad arms twenty fathom wide —
That is to say, the branches had been laid

On such a space.   But first was straw conveyed
And strewn about.   Yet how the pyre arose
So high, and what were all the trees they chose,
As willow, plane-tree, fir, birch, alder, yew,
Poplar, elm, ash, oak (with the holm-oak too),
Maple, thorn, beech, asp, hazel, cornel-tree,
Laurel, box, linden, chestnut — shall not be
Told here, nor how the gods in agitation
Ran up and down, robbed of their habitation,
The gods that dwelt in peace and silence here —
Nymphs, fauns, and hamadryads; nor the fear
Of all the animals and birds that fled
When the green woodland was deforested,
Nor how the ground aghast was of the light
That never had known the glare of sunshine bright,
Nor how the pyre with straw at first was laid,
Then high with dry and broken limbs was made,
And then with green wood and with spicery,
And then with cloth of gold and jewelry,
And flower with flower in woven garlands blent,
And myrrh and incense breathing heavy scent,
Nor how amid all this Arcita lay,
With riches set beside him on display,
Nor how, as was the custom, Emely
Put in the funeral fire, how later she
Fell in a swoon when they had made the fire;
Nor what she said, nor what was her desire,
Nor what of jewels in the flame were cast,
When it was great of size and burning fast,
Nor how some cast the shields and spears they bore,
And some threw in the vestments that they wore,
And cups of wine and blood and milk they had

Into the fire that burned as it were mad;
Nor how the Greeks in great procession turned
Leftwards around the fire the while it burned,
Three times, and how they raised a mighty shout
And thrice their lances as they marched about
Clashed; nor of how the ladies thrice did cry,
Nor of the leading home of Emely,
Nor how to ashes cold was burned Arcite,
Nor how they held the body-wake all night
Unto the dawn, and how the Athenians played
The wake-plays — all of this I leave unsaid;
Nor who was entered in the wrestling test
Naked and oiled, nor who was judged the best
Will I say now — nor how they all are gone
Homeward to Athens when the sport is done —
But quickly to the point will come instead
And thereby get my long tale wholly said.

By process and by length of certain years
Stayed wholly are the mourning and the tears
Of all the Greeks, by general assent,
And then I think there was a parliament
At Athens, that for certain matters met,
Among which matters was the question set
To make with certain countries an alliance,
And get from Thebes obedience and compliance.
And royal Theseus, working to this end,
Soon after noble Palamon doth send,
And he knew not the wherefore or the why,
But in his sable raiment mournfully
Straight at the word of Theseus cometh he.
Then Theseus sent at once for Emely.
When all were seated there, and hushed the place,

And Theseus sat in silence for a space
Ere any wise word sounded from his breast,
There where he chose he fixed his eyes at rest,
And sighed with a sad visage, quietly,
And after that his will thus uttered he.
  "The primal Mover and First Cause above,
When first He made the beauteous chain of love,
Great was the end, and great was His intent;
Well knew He why, well knew He what he meant.
Of that fair chain of love He made a band
Holding the air, the flame, the flood, the land
In definite boundaries, that they might not flee.
That Mover and that self-same Prince," said he,
"Hath set below here in this vile creation
Limits of certain days as a duration
For all things that are born within this place,
Beyond which day they may not go a pace
Though certainly they may their terms abridge.
Nor need we here authority allege,
For by experience we prove it well.
But let me briefly now my meaning tell —
By this arrangement, then, may all men see
Firm is this Mover, for eternity.
Now all know well, unless it be a fool,
That every part deriveth from its whole.
For surely nature never took her start
From any fragment of a thing, or part,
But something perfect, standing firm and well,
Till it became with time corruptible.
And therefore, working with a wise intent,
He hath so well ordained his government
That all progressions and all species known

In their successions shall endure alone —
Not be eternal, and no issue leave.
This ye may know and well by eye perceive.
    "For lo ! the oak, whose growth is always slow
From the first day when it begins to grow,
And hath so long a life, as we may see —
Yet in the end comes Death and takes the tree.
    "Consider, too, the hard unyielding stone
Under our feet, where men have come and gone —
It wears to waste as by the road it lies;
And broadest river on occasion dries.
We watch great cities changing, vanishing —
So we behold an end for everything.
    "Nor less must men and women, as we know,
Like these, and in one season of the two —
That is to say, in youth, or else in age,
Be dead at last, the king beside the page;
One in his bed and one at sea may go,
And one in battle pass, as all men know;
Nothing avails, all take the self-same way,
And all this world must perish, I may say.
Who causeth this but Jupiter the king ?
He that is prince and cause of everything,
And re-converteth all things to the source
From which, in truth, they came and took their course.
Against this fate no creature that hath life,
Whatever kind, makes more than futile strife.
    "Then it is wisdom, as it seems to me,
To make a virtue of necessity,
And take it well, nor shun what may befall,
Especially the things that come to all.
And who complains, he maketh but a folly,

And rebel is to Him that guides us wholly.
And honor gives that man the greatest dower
Who comes to death in excellence and flower,
When he hath certitude of goodly name;
Then hath he done nor friend nor self a shame.
And happier should his friend be in his death
When yielded up with honor goes his breath
Than when with age a withered name appears,
And all his prowess dies upon the years.
Then it is best for nobleness of fame,
That he should die when he is best of name.
To oppose this is but wilful.   Why should we
Complain, why do we look so mournfully
That good Arcite, of chivalry the flower,
With honor and with duty at his hour
Hath left the wretched prison of this life ?
And why lament his cousin and his wife
Whom he hath loved so well, about his lot ?
What — can he thank them ?   God knows ! — not a jot !
Since they his soul and their own selves offend,
And yet their happiness nowise amend.
  "What comes of all this lengthy argument
But I advise we turn to merriment
After our grief, and thank Jove for his grace ?
And I advise, before we leave the place,
That we should fashion, of two sorrows sore,
One perfect gladness lasting evermore;
And let us see where sorrow gnaws the worst —
There will we undertake our mending first !
  "Sister," said he, "this is my whole intent,
With full accord of all my parliament —
That noble Palamon, who is your knight,

That serveth you with will and heart and might,
And ever hath, since first that ye did know him —
That ye shall now your grace and pity show him,
And take him for your husband and your lord;
Give me your hand, for this is our accord.
Now of your woman's pity let me see !
By God, a king's own brother's son is he,
And though a landless bachelor he were,
Since he hath been for years your servitor,
And such adversity for you endured,
This must be well considered, be assured;
For noble mercy ought to conquer fully."
    And then this Palamon addressing duly,
"I think a scanty sermon," he began,
"Will win us your agreement to this plan.
Come near and take your lady's hand."   And so
Straightway the bond was made between the two
Called marriage, that was witnessed solemnly
By all the council and nobility.
Thus with all bliss and joyous melody
This Palamon hath wedded Emely.
And God, that all this mighty world hath wrought,
Send him his love, that hath it dearly bought.
For Palamon may count all blessings his,
Living in health and riches and in bliss,
And Emely loveth him so tenderly,
And he serves her with such nobility,
That never a word there was between the two
Of jealousy — nor other grief they knew.
And thus end Palamon and Emely,
And God save all this goodly company.

Amen.

The Prioress's Tale

The Prioress's Tale

THERE was in Asia, in a city great,
Mid Christian folk, a Jewish colony,
Protected by a lord who ruled that state,
For wicked gain and foulest usury,
Hateful to Christ and to His company;
And through the street all men could walk or ride;
For it was free, with both ends open wide.

A little school of Christian people stood
Down at the farther end, in which there were
Children full many come of Christian blood
That studied in that school from year to year
The kind of lessons taught to students there —
Singing, that is to say, and reading too,
Such things as children in their childhood do.

Among these children was a widow's son —
A little chorister but seven years old;
Who day by day to school had always gone;
And any time he might the form behold
Of Jesu's mother, then, as he was schooled,
It was his custom down to kneel and say
His *Ave Maria* as he went his way.

The widow thus her little son had taught
Always to worship Christ's own mother dear,
Lady of bliss; and nowise he forgot,
For a good child is quick of eye and ear,
But when I call to mind this story here,
St. Nicholas himself appears to me,
For he when young served Christ so reverently.

This little child, while studying among
The others in the school was soon aware
Of *Alma Redemptoris* being sung
By children that were learning anthems there;
And ever he edged as close as he might dare,
And listened to the singing, word and note,
Until he had the whole first verse by rote.

Nothing he knew of what this Latin said,
Being too tender in his years, and young,
But with a comrade on a day he plead
To explain this song to him in his own tongue,
Or tell him wherefore it was being sung;
To know the words and what was meant by these
Eager and oft he prayed him on bare knees.

His comrade was an older boy than he,
And answered thus: "This song, I hear folk say,
Was made about our blissful Lady free,
To hail and give her greeting, and to pray
Her help and grace when we shall pass away.
No more about the matter can I tell;
Singing I learn, but grammar not so well."

"And is this song made then in reverence
Of Christ's dear mother ?" cried this innocent;

"Now truly, I will make great diligence
To know it all, ere Christmastide be spent,
Though in my work I suffer punishment
And thrice an hour be beaten for it," said he,
"Yet will I learn it, honoring our Lady."

Each day his fellow taught him privately
While going home, until he knew by rote
The whole, and sang it well and lustily
From word to word, according to the note,
And twice a day the song would pass his throat,
Once when to school and once when home he went;
On Christ's dear mother was his whole intent.

This child passed through the Jewish colony,
As I have said, in going to and fro,
And there full merry would he sing, and cry
"*O Alma Redemptoris;*" for the glow
And sweetness pierced his little spirit so
Of Christ's dear mother, that he could not stay
His song to pray to her along the way.

Satan, that serpent and our ancient foe,
That hath in Jewish heart his hornet's nest,
Swelled up and cried, "Woe, Hebrew people, woe !
In such dishonor do ye dwell at rest ?
Must ye endure these accents ye detest,
Hearing this boy that goes with evil cause
To desecrate by song your faith and laws ?"

And from that day the wicked Jews conspired
How they could bring this innocent to die,

And to this end a homicide they hired
That had his dwelling in an alley nigh,
And as the little child was going by,
This Jew leapt forth and seized him fast, and slit
His throat, and cast his body in a pit.

Into a privy they his body threw,
Where all these Jews had purged them commonly,
O cursed folk, O Herods born anew,
What shall avail you all your infamy ?
Murder will out; yea, this is certainty;
And where God's honor lifteth voice to plead,
Loud cries the blood against your cursèd deed !

O martyr wedded to virginity
Now mayst thou sing indeed, and follow on
After the white celestial Lamb (cried she);
Of thee the great evangelist, St. John
In Patmos wrote, saying of martyrs gone
Before the Lamb, and singing songs all new,
That never women in the flesh they knew !

This widow sat awaiting all the night
Her little child, and yet he cometh not;
So when the day drew once again to light,
Her face all pale with fear and heavy thought
At school and every place about she sought,
Until thus much she learned at length — that he
Was seen last in the Jewish colony.

With mother's pity burning in her breast,
She goes as if she had but half her mind,

To every place where there could be the least
Of likelihood her little child to find;
And ever on Christ's mother meek and kind
She called, and so at length, and long distraught,
Among the cursèd Jews her child she sought.

She asketh and she prayeth piteously
Of all the Jews that dwelt within that place,
To tell her if they saw her child go by,
And they said "No."   But Jesu, of His grace,
This impulse gave her in a little space:
That for her little son she stood and cried
Where he within the pit lay close beside.

O mighty God, who let'st Thy praise be called
By mouths of innocents, lo, here Thy might !
This gem of chastity, this emerald
Of martyrdom, this blessèd ruby bright,
There where he lay with throat all gashed and white,
"*O Alma Redemptoris*" clearly sang —
So loud that all the place about him rang.

The Christians on the street, that came and went,
Rushed up with wonder as they heard him sing,
And for the provost hastily they sent;
And he came thither without tarrying,
And Christ he praised that is of heaven the King,
And His dear mother, glory of mankind;
And after that, the Jews he bade them bind.

This little child with piteous lamentation
Was lifted up the while he sang his song,

And, honored by a mighty congregation,
Unto the nearest abbey borne along;
There by the bier his mother swooning hung,
And scarcely could the people that were there
This second Rachel from his body tear.

This provost bade at once that every Jew
With torture and by shameful death should die
That anything about this murder knew;
He would not tolerate such iniquity;
Evil to them where evil ought to lie !
So first he had them dragged behind wild horses,
Then hanged: the judgment which the law enforces.

Upon his bier still lay this innocent
By the chief altar while the mass was said
And after that, the priests and abbot went
With all dispatch to burial of the dead;
But sprinkling holy water on his head,
They heard him speak, at sprinkling of the water,
And sing — "*O Alma Redemptoris Mater !*"

Now this good abbot was a holy man,
As all monks are (or leastwise ought to be !)
And so to conjure this young child began,
And said, "Beloved child, I ask of thee,
By virtue of the Holy Trinity,
Tell me the reason why, though it appear
Thy throat is cut, thou singest still so clear."

"My throat is cut, yea, to the very bone,"
Answered this child, "and following nature's way,

Long time ago I should have died and gone,
But Jesu Christ, as find ye books to say,
Wills that His glory be in mind, and stay,
And so for honor of His mother dear,
Still may I sing O *Alma* loud and clear.

"Always I loved Christ's Mother, well of grace,
My wit and knowledge wholly thus applying,
And when they threw my body in that place,
She came to me and spoke as I was lying,
And bade me sing this song when I was dying,
As ye have heard, and, after I had sung,
I thought she laid a grain upon my tongue.

"Therefore I sing, and sing I must indeed,
In honor of that sainted maiden free,
Till from my tongue ye take away the seed;
And afterwards these words she said to me:
'My little child, I will come back for thee
When from thy tongue the grain at last is taken;
Be not dismayed, thou shalt not be forsaken.'"

This holy monk, this abbot, instantly
Drew out the tongue and took away the grain,
And he gave up his spirit quietly;
And when the abbot saw this wonder plain,
His salt tears trickled down his cheeks like rain,
Face down he fell all flat upon the ground,
And lay there still as he with cords were bound.

And all the convent on the pavement lay
Weeping and praising Christ's own mother dear,

And after that they rose and went away
Taking this blessed martyr from his bier
And made for him a tomb of marble clear,
And in it closed his little body sweet;
Where he is now, pray God we all shall meet !

O Hugh of Lincoln, slain in youth also
By cursèd Jews, as all the world knows well,
For it was but a little time ago,
Pray too for us, sinful and changeable,
That God, in whom abounding mercies dwell,
May multiply His grace on us, and thence
Do to His mother Mary reverence !

The Nun's Priest's Tale

The Nun's Priest's Tale

ONCE, long ago, set close beside a wood,
Meagre of look, a little cottage stood
Where dwelt a poor old widow in a dale.
This widow, she of whom I tell my tale,
Even since the day when she was last a wife
All patiently had led a simple life;
Small were her earnings and her property,
But what God sent she used with husbandry,
And kept two daughters and herself.   Of sows
Three and no more she had about the house,
Also a sheep called Molly, and three kine.
Her sooty hall and bower were nothing fine,
And there full many a slender meal she ate.
No poignant sauce was needed for her plate;
No dainty morsel passed her throat; her fare
Accorded with the clothes she had to wear.
With surfeit she was never sick, but in
A temperate diet was her medicine,
And busy labor, and a heart's content.
Gout never kept her from a dance; nor bent
With stroke of apoplexy was her head.
Of wine none drank she, neither white nor red;
Her board was mostly served with white and black:

Milk and brown bread; of these she found no lack;
And bacon, or an egg, was not uncommon,
For in her way she was a dairywoman.
　　She had a yard, that was enclosed about
By sticks, and a dry ditch that ran without,
And there she kept a cock named Chanticleer;
None in the land at crowing was his peer.
His voice was merrier than the organ's tone
That loud on mass-days in the church is blown,
And surer from his lodge his crowing fell
Than stroke of any clock or abbey bell.
He knew by nature each ascension of
The equinoxial circle arched above,
For when fifteen degrees had been ascended,
He crowed, so that it could not be amended.
Redder than coral was his comb, and all
Crested with notches, like a castle wall;
His bill was black — like jet it seemed to glow —
Like azure shone each leg and every toe,
His nails were white — the lily flower is duller;
And gold all burnished was his body's color.
This noble cock had under governance
Seven hens, to do all wholly his pleasance;
Which were his paramours and sisters dear
And in their colors matched him wondrous near;
Of whom she that was fairest hued of throat
Fairly was called, Damoselle Pertelote.
Courteous she was, discreet and debonaire,
Companionable, and bore herself so fair
Even since the day that she was seven nights old,
She hath the heart of Chanticleer in hold —
Locked in each motion, in each graceful limb;

He loved her so, that this was well with him.
But what a joy it was to hear them sing
In sweet accord: "My Love's Gone Journeying"
While the bright sun uprose from out the land,
For this was in the time, I understand,
When all the birds and beasts could sing and speak.
　So once it fell, as day began to break,
And Chanticleer with his wives one and all
Was sitting on his perch within the hall,
And next him sat this fair Dame Pertelote,
That Chanticleer groaned deeply in his throat,
Like one that in his dream sore troubled is.
And when she heard this roaring groan of his,
Pertelote was aghast, and cried: "Dear heart,
What aileth you, that thus ye groan and start?
What a fine sleeper!　Fie now, fie for shame!"
But Chanticleer replied: "I pray you, Dame,
Take it not so amiss; by God, I seemed
Just now in such a danger as I dreamed
That still my heart it shuddereth with fright.
Now God," he cried, "expound my dream aright,
And out of prison foul my body keep!
Now I was roaming (so I dreamed in sleep)
Within our yard, and there I saw a beast
Was like a dog, and would have made arrest
Upon my body, and would have had me dead.
His color was between a yellow and red,
And tipped his tail was, likewise both his ears,
With black, quite different from his other hairs.
His snout was small between two glowing eyes;
Even now my heart with terror almost dies;
And doubtless it was this which made me start."

"For shame !" quoth she, "Fie on you, small of heart !
Alas !" she cried, "for, by the God above,
Now have ye lost my heart and all my love:
I cannot love a coward, by my faith.
For truly, what so any woman saith,
We all desire, if such a thing can be,
Husbands that shall be sturdy, wise, and free,
Trusty, and not a fool, nor one to hoard,
Nor such as stands aghast to see a sword,
Nor yet a boaster, by the God above:
How durst ye say for shame unto your love
That there was anything on earth ye feared ?
Have ye no man's heart, though ye have a beard ?
And was it dreams that brought this melancholy ?
God knows that nothing is in dreams but folly.
Dreams are engendered out of gluttony,
And drink, and from complexions, it may be,
That show of humors more than should be right.
Surely this vision which ye dreamed last night
Comes of the too great superfluity
Ye have of your red *colera,* pardee,
Which makes folk in their dreams to have great dread
Of arrows, or of fire with tongues of red,
Of great beasts, that will bite them, and of all
Struggle and strife, and dogs both great and small —
Just as the humor of melancholy will make
Full many a man within his sleep to break
Out crying with fear of black bears or black bulls
Or else of some black devil that at him pulls.
Of other humors I could tell you still
That work on many a sleeping man much ill,
But I will pass as quickly as I can.

"Lo, Cato, he that was so wise a man,
Said he not thus: Take no account of dreams ?
Now sire," she said, "when we fly from the beams
For God's love take a little laxative;
Upon my soul, and as I hope to live,
My counsel is the best, and it is wholly
The truth: for choler and for melancholy
Purge yourself now; and, since ye must not tarry,
And in this town is no apothecary,
I will myself to certain herbs direct you
That shall be profit to you, and correct you;
And in our very yard such herbs should be
Which of their nature have the property
To purge you wholly, under and above.
Forget this not, I say, for God's own love !
Ye are too choleric of complexion;
Then take good heed lest the ascending sun
Shall find you all replete with humors hot;
For if it do, I dare to lay a groat
That ye shall straightway have a tertian fever
Or ague, that may be your bane forever.
A day or two ye shall your diet make
On worms, and then your laxatives shall take:
Spurge-laurel, for example, and centaury
And fumitory, or hellebore, may be,
With caper-spurge, too, or the gaytree berry,
And in our yard ground ivy that makes merry.
Just peck them where they grow, and eat.   But make
Good cheer now, husband, for your fathers' sake.
Fear ye no dream; now can I say no more."

"Madam," quoth he, "*Graunt mercy* for your lore.
Yet touching this Lord Cato who, I own,

Hath for his wisdom such a great renown,
Though he adviseth us to take no heed
Of dreams — by God, in old books can ye read
Of many a man, more in authority
Than ever Cato was, God prosper me,
That say just the reverse of what he says,
And by experience in many ways
Find that our dreams may be prophetic things
Alike for joys and woeful happenings
That in this present life all folk endure.
This needs no argument to make it sure,
For the full proof is shown in many a deed.

    "One of the greatest authors that men read
Says thus: that on a time two friends set out
On pilgrimage, and they were both devout;
And it befell they came unto a town
Where were such crowds of people up and down
And in the hostelries so little space
There was not even a cottage in the place
Wherein the both of them might harbored be.
So they were forced, of sheer necessity,
For that night's sleeping to part company,
And each of them goes to his hostelry
To take his lodging as it might befall.
The one of them was bedded in a stall
Out in a yard with oxen of the plow;
The other got a proper place somehow,
As was his chance, or fortune, it may be,
That all lives governs universally.

    "And it befell that, long before the day,
This man, as dreaming in his bed he lay,
Thought that he heard his friend begin him call,

Crying: 'Alas ! for in an ox's stall
This night shall I be murdered as I lie.
Now help me, dear my brother, ere I die.
Arise ! in all haste come to me !' he said.
His comrade started from his sleep in dread,
But when he was awakened from his dreaming
He turned, and gave no notice to it, deeming
That all his dream was but a vanity !
And twice as he was sleeping thus dreamed he.
And then he thought he saw his friend again
A third time, and he said, 'Now am I slain.
Behold my wounds, bloody and deep and wide !
Arise up early on the morrow-tide
And at the west gate of the town,' quoth he,
'A cart with dung full laden shalt thou see,
In which my body is hidden secretly;
Then boldly stop that dung-cart instantly.
My gold did cause my murder, to say truly.'
Then all the slaying did he tell him duly,
With a full piteous face and pale of hue.
And ye may trust, his dream he found full true.
For on the morrow, with the break of day,
Unto his comrade's inn he took his way,
And when he came upon the ox's stall
To his companion he began to call.

   "The landlord spoke and answered him anon
After this fashion: 'Sir, your friend is gone;
He went from out the town when day first broke.'
Then straightway in this man suspicion woke,
For he remembered what he dreamed, and he
Would stay no more, but went forth instantly
Unto the west gate of the town, and found

A dung-cart, set as if to dung the ground,
That was arrayed exactly in the way
As in his dream he heard the dead man say.
Then with a bold heart he began to cry
Justice and vengeance on this villany:
'My friend was slain last night, and in this cart
Lies staring with a wound above his heart !
I cry upon the officers,' quoth he,
'That should keep rule here, and security !
Help ! Help ! Alas, here lies my comrade slain !'
What should I add to make the tale more plain ?
The folk rushed out and cast the cart to ground,
And in the middle of the dung they found
The body of the man, murdered all new.

"O blissful God, that art so just and true !
Lo ! always thus murder dost thou betray !
Murder will out, we see it day by day.
So loathsome is it, and such cursèd treason
To God, the soul of justice and of reason,
That never will He let it hidden be;
Though it should stay a year or two or three,
Murder will out — this is my whole opinion.
Straightway the officers that had dominion
Over the city, seized and tortured so
The carter, and the hostler with him, too,
That soon they both confessed their villainy
And by the neck were hanged.

               "So men may see
From such examples, dreams are to be feared.
And truly, in the same book there appeared,
Right in the chapter following on this
(I lie not, as I hope for joy or bliss)

A tale of two that would have left the strand
To cross the sea and reach a far-off land
If the wind's motion had not been contrary,
But in a city this had made them tarry
That stood full pleasant by a harbor-side.
But finally, one day, toward eventide,
The wind made change; right as they wished it blew,
Then happy to their slumber went the two
With hope full early to be voyaging.
But unto one befell a marvellous thing,
For, in his sleep, almost at break of day,
He had a wondrous vision as he lay.
It seemed to him a man stood at his side
Warning him in that city to abide,
Saying: 'If thou tomorrow go thy way
Thou shalt be drowned; I have no more to say.'
He woke, and told his vision to his friend,
And prayed him, lest the dream some ill portend,
To put the voyage off beyond that morn.
At that his friend began to laugh in scorn
Lying the while near by within his bed,
'No dream shall ruin my affairs,' he said,
'Stirring my fears with fancies wild and teeming.
I wouldn't give a straw for all thy dreaming.
Vain tricks are dreams wherethrough the mind escapes
To fashion fantasies of owls or apes,
And many a maze. By God, for certainty,
Men dream what never was and cannot be.
But since I see that thou art bent on staying,
Wasting thy time with visions and delaying,
God knows I am sorry for it — so good day.'
And thus he took his leave and went his way.

But it befell ere half his course was sailed,
I know not why, nor what mischance assailed,
By accident his vessel's hull was rent,
And ship and man beneath the water went
In sight of other ships not far away
That at the same time sailed with them that day.
Therefore, my fair, belovèd Pertelote,
From such old stories mayst thou clearly note
That no man should too greatly scoff about
His dreams; indeed, I tell thee, out of doubt
Full many a dream deserveth well our dread.

"Lo, lately in Saint Kenelm's life I read —
That was Kenulphus' son, the noble king
Of Mercia, how young Kenelm dreamed a thing.
One night, a little time ere he was killed,
His murder in a vision he beheld.
His nurse explained this vision well unto him,
And warned him of the treason men might do him,
And bade him be on guard; yet having but seven
Years only, and a heart all fixed on heaven,
To any vision little heed gave he.
By God, but it were worth my shirt to me
If thou hadst read this, Madam, as have I.
Dame Pertelote, I tell thee truthfully,
Macrobeus, that wrote down long ago
In Africa the dream of Scipio
Commendeth dreams, and says they often be
Warnings of things that afterwards men see.

"And furthermore, I pray you notice well
In the Old Testament, if Daniël
Believed that dreams were any vanity,
And read of Joseph too, and ye shall see

Whether some dreams may be (I say not all)
Warnings of things that afterwards befall.
Consider Egypt's King, Dan Pharao,
And mark his baker and his butler, too,
Whether of dreams they felt not the result.
Whoso will divers histories consult
May read of dreams full many a wondrous thing.
    "Lo, Crœsus, that in Lydia was king, —
Did he not dream he sat upon a tree,
Which signified his hanging that should be ?
And lo, Andromache, Dan Hector's wife —
Before the day that Hector lost his life
Dreams gave her warning that should Hector go
With day to join the fight against the foe,
The life of Hector would be lost, and she
Warned him of this, but unsuccessfully.
He went to fight, holding her vision vain,
And so was shortly by Achilles slain.
But this tale is too long to tell, and dawn
Draws near already; I may not go on.
In brief, and for conclusion, I assert
That of this vision I shall have some hurt.
And Madam, I will tell you furthermore
That on these laxatives I set no store,
For they are venomous, I'll never try them;
I love them never a jot, and I defy them !
 · "Now let us speak of mirth, and stop all this;
Dame Pertelote, as I have hope of bliss,
In one thing God hath richly sent me grace,
For when I see the beauty of your face
Ye be so scarlet red about the eyes
That as I gaze all dread within me dies,

For sure as gospel I would have you know,
Mulier est hominis confusio;
Madam, the meaning of this Latin is —
Woman's the joy of man and all his bliss.
For when at night I feel your fluffy side,
Although I may not then upon you ride,
Because our perch, alas, is made so narrow,
Such joy and solace pierce me to the marrow
That then do I defy both vision and dream."
And with that word he flew down from the beam —
For it was day — and his hens one and all;
And with a chucking he commenced to call,
For in the yard he had found a grain of corn.
His fear he scorned now with a royal scorn;
He feathered Pertelote full twenty time,
And trod as often, ere that it was prime.
All like unto a lion grim he goes,
And strutteth up and down upon his toes.
Scarcely he deigned with foot to touch the ground,
And chucked all proudly when a corn he found,
And then his wives ran to him, one and all.
Thus royal, like a prince within his hall,
Here of this Chanticleer I take farewell,
And after of his danger will I tell.

Now when the month in which the world began,
That March is called, when God first fashioned man,
Was all completed — yea, and more than through —
Since March had started, thirty days and two —
It fell that Chanticleer, in all his pride,
His wives all seven walking by his side,
Cast his eye upward to the shining sun
That in the sign of Taurus now had run

Twenty and one degrees and somewhat more,
And knew by nature (and no other lore)
That it was prime, and crew out lustily.
And, "Now the sun has climbed the heaven," said he,
"Forty degrees and one, and more for sure;
Dame Pertelote, my bliss and paramour,
Hearken these birds how joyfully they sing,
And see the flowers, how fresh and bright they spring;
Full is my heart of joy and revelling."
But suddenly befell a grievous thing,
For ever the farther end of joy is woe.
God know'th that joys of earth are soon to go,
And if an orator could write this well,
He might embed it in a chronicle
As a fact of sovereign notability.
Let every wise man listen unto me;
This story is just as true, I undertake,
As is the book of Launcelot of the Lake,
Whereof are ladies reverent and fain;
Now to my theme will I return again.
    A black-marked fox, wicked and very sly,
Had lurked for three years in the wood near by,
And by a fine, premeditated plot
That same night, breaking through the hedge, had got
Into the yard where Chanticleer the fair
Was with his wives accustomed to repair;
And in a bed of herbs stone-still he lay
Till onward to eleven went the day,
Waiting his time on Chanticleer to fall
As do the murderers gladly — one and all —
That low in ambush crouch to murder men.
O treacherous murderer, lurking in thy den !

O new Iscariot ! O new Ganilon !
O false dissembler, O thou Greek Sinon
That broughtest Troy all utterly to sorrow !
O Chanticleer, accursèd be that morrow
That thou into the yard flew from the beams.
Thou hadst been well admonished in thy dreams
That this same day was perilous to thee.
But that which God foreknows must surely be
As certain scholars make the matter work.
This ye will learn from any well-trained clerk:
Upon that point has been great altercation
Within the schools, and lengthy disputation
Among a hundred thousand if a man !
But I could never sift it to the bran
As could the holy doctor Augustine,
Or Boëthius, or Bishop Brandwardine
To say if God's divine forewitnessing
Compelleth me of need to do a thing
(By need I mean simple necessity)
Or whether a free choice be granted me
To do that same thing or to do it not,
Though God foreknew it ere that it was wrought;
Or if his knowing binds me not a whit,
Save on condition, to accomplish it !
In no such matters will I interfere;
My tale is of a cock, as ye may hear,
That from his wife took counsel, to his sorrow,
To walk within the yard upon that morrow
That he had dreamed the dream I have related.
Women's advice is oftentimes ill-fated !
Counsel of woman brought us first to woe
And out of Paradise made Adam go

Though he was merry there, and well at ease.
But since I know not whom it might displease
Should I the advice of women hold to blame —
Forget it, for I said it but in game.
Read authors where they treat of such affairs
And hear of women in these books of theirs;
These are the cock's words only, none of mine,
For in no woman can I harm divine !

Fair in the sand, to bathe her merrily
Lieth Pertelote, with all her sisters nigh
In the warm sun, and Chanticleer so free,
Sung merrier than the mermaid in the sea;
(Physiologus says for certainty
That they sing very well and merrily).
And so it fell that, as he cast his eye
Among the worts, upon a butterfly,
He saw this fox before him, crouching low.
Nowise it pleased him then to strut or crow,
But quick "Cok, Cok" he cried, and up he started
Like one fear striketh suddenly weak-hearted.
For any creature will desire to flee
If suddenly his enemy he see,
Though never before he saw it with his eye.

This Chanticleer, when he the fox did spy,
He would have fled, but that the fox anon
Said, "Noble sire, alas ! will ye be gone ?
Be ye afraid of me that am your friend ?
Now truly, I were worse than any fiend
If I should plan you hurt or villainy.
I did not come your secrets to espy;
Surely, the one and only reason bringing
Me here — it was to listen to your singing.

For certainly ye have as merry a steven
As any angel hath that sings in heaven;
There is more feeling in your music than
Boethius had, or any singing man.
My lord your father (God him sanctify)
Likewise your mother (in her great courtesy)
Have been within my house, to my great ease,
And truly, sire, full fain I would you please.
But with respect to singing, in this wise
I say: that as I hope to keep my eyes
I never heard such singing from a man
As from your father when the day began —
Truly, it was full lusty, all his song;
And that his voice might ring more clear and strong
He used to strain until his eyes would close,
So loudly would he cry; and he uprose
Upon his toe tips as he crowed withal,
And stretched his neck out very long and small.
He was of such discretion, too, that there
Was none in any country anywhere
That him in song or wisdom might surpass.
True, I have read in Dan Burnell the Ass,
Among his verse, how that there was a cock
Who, all because a priest's son gave a knock
Unto his leg when he was young, — for this
Schemed that he later lost his benefice;
But certainly, no man can well compare
The high discretion and the wisdom rare
Your father had, with that cock's trickery.
But now sing, sire, sing for Saint Charity;
Try now, can ye your father counterfeit?"
This Chanticleer his wings began to beat

As one that could no treachery descry —
So was he ravished by this flattery.

Alas ! ye lords, full many false rogue is there
Within your courts, and many a flatterer,
That please you often more, upon my faith,
Than he that ever the truth unto you saith.
Read the Ecclesiast on flattery;
Beware, ye lordlings, of their treachery !

This Chanticleer stood high upon his toes,
He stretched his neck, he made his eyes to close,
And thus began to make a mighty cry.
Sir Russell Fox up-bounded instantly
And by the throat he seized this Chanticleer,
And flung him on his back, and sped from there
Off toward the wood, and no man saw him run.
O Destiny, that none of us may shun !
Alas ! that Chanticleer flew from the beams !
Alas ! that Pertelote recked not of dreams !
And on a Friday fell all this mischance !
O Venus, that art goddess of pleasance,
Since Chanticleer was servant unto thee
And spent himself to serve thee faithfully,
More for delight than the world to multiply,
Why wouldst thou suffer him on thy day to die ?
O Geoffrey, master dear and highly skilled,
That when King Richard was with arrow killed
Made for thy noble lord complaint so sore,
Why do I lack thy meaning and thy lore,
Friday to chide with singing, as did ye ?
(For truly, on a Friday slain was he).
Then would I raise my sorrowful refrain
For Chanticleer's affright, and for his pain.

Not such a lamentation and great crying
Did Trojan ladies make for Ilium dying,
When fire and Pyrrhus' naked sword they feared,
Who seized the aged Priam by the beard
And slew him (so the Æneid tells the tale)
As did these hens that in the yard made wail
To see their Chanticleer in fearsome plight.
But Pertelote shrieked with surpassing might;
Louder she cried than did Hasdrubal's wife
What time she saw Hasdrubal lose his life
And Carthage burned by Roman torches. She
Was filled with grief and torment utterly,
And in the fire she flung herself, and so
Steadfast of heart in flames to death did go.
O woeful hens, your cry was like the cry
When Nero sent Rome City to the sky
And there was fearful wailing from the wives
Of Roman senators that lost their lives;
All guiltless, wicked Nero had them slain !
Now to my tale will I return again.

This simple widow and her daughters two
Heard all these hens lament with great to-do,
And rushing out of doors at once, they see
The fox make toward the forest hastily
Bearing the cock away upon his back.
They cried: "Out !" "Harrow !" "Welaway !" "Alack !"
"Ha ! Ha ! the fox !" and after him they ran,
And with them waving sticks came many a man;
And Collie our dog and Talbot and Gerland,
And Malkin, with a distaff in her hand;
The cows and calves ran, and the very hogs,
Crazed as they were with the barking of the dogs

And men and women making great halloo;
Their hearts with running all but burst in two.
They yelled like fiends in hell — who could have stilled
    them ?
And the ducks cried as someone would have killed them.
The geese for fear went flying over trees,
Out of the hive there poured a swarm of bees;
Ah ! *Benedicite !* such wild noise rang
In truth, that Jack Straw ramping with his gang
In search of some poor Fleming they could kill
Never made shouting that was half so shrill
As on that day was made about this fox.
They came with trumpets made of brass and box,
Of horn and bone on which they blew and tooted,
And therewithal they shrieked and whooped and hooted
Until it seemed that heaven itself would fall.
And now, good men, I pray you hearken all !
    Look now how fortune turneth suddenly
The hope and triumph of their enemy.
This cock, upon the fox's back that lay,
Despite his fear, still found a voice to say
Thus to the fox: "Now, sire, were I as ye,
God help me, I would shout defiantly:
'Turn once again, proud churls, turn one and all !
A very pestilence upon you fall !
Look ye, at last I stand within the wood !
Now do your worst, the cock is mine for good,
For I will eat him up, and quickly, too.' "
The fox replied: "In faith, that will I do !" —
But as he spoke the word, the cock broke free
Out of his open mouth full dextrously
And flew high up and perched upon a limb.

And the fox saw him there and called to him:
"Alas ! O Chanticleer, alas !" quoth he,
"I fear that I have done you injury !
I frightened you by seizing you so hard
And rushing with you hither from your yard;
But sire, I did it with no ill intent —
Come down, and I will tell you what I meant.
I will speak truth to you, God help me so."
"Nay, then," quoth he, "my curse upon us two,
And first I'll curse myself, both blood and bones,
If thou shalt fool me oftener than once !
Thou shalt no more with crafty flatteries
Make me to sing for thee and close my eyes.
For he who shuts his eyes when he should see —
God give no good to any such as he !"
"Nay," quoth the fox, "but God give him mischance
That is so indiscreet of governance
That jabbers when he ought to hold his tongue !"
   So of the negligent my tale is sung,
That reckless are, and trust in flattery.
But if ye deem this naught but vanity,
As of a fox, or of a cock and hen,
Take ye the moral that it hath, good men.
For Saint Paul, saith he not that all things writ
Can point our doctrine and embellish it ?
Then take the grain and let the chaff lie still.
And now, good God, if it shall be thy will
As saith my lord, so make us all good men
And bring us into holy bliss. *Amen.*

The Pardoner's Tale

The Pardoner's Tale

Now these three rioters of whom I tell,
Long yet ere prime was rung by any bell,
Were seated in a tavern at their drinking.
And as they sat, they heard a death-bell clinking
Before a body going to its grave.
Then roused the one and shouted to his knave —
"Be off at once !" he cried.   "Run out and spy
Whose body it may be that passeth by;
And look thou get his name aright," he cried.

   "No need, sir — none at all," this boy replied.
"They told me that before ye came, two hours;
He was, God's name, an old fellow of yours.
By night, it seems, and sudden was his dying;
Flat on his bench, all drunken, was he lying,
When up there crept a thief that men call Death
(Who in this country all the people slay'th)
And smote his heart asunder with his spear
And all in silence went his way from here.
During the plague he hath a thousand slain,
And master, ere ye meet him this is plain:
That it is wise and very necessary
To be prepared for such an adversary,

Have readiness to meet him evermore;
So taught my mother — now I say no more."
"Yea, by Saint Mary," said the taverner,
"The boy speaks true, for he hath slain this year
Woman and child and man in yonder town,
And page and villain he hath smitten down.
I hold his habitation must be there.
Great wisdom were it that a man beware —
Lest he some fearful injury incur."
"Yea, by God's arms," replied this rioter.
"Is he so perilous a knave to meet ?
Now will I seek him both by way and street,
Upon the bones of God I make a vow !
Fellows, we three are one — then hear me now:
Let each of us hold up his hand to th' other,
And each of us become the other's brother;
And we will slay this faithless traitor Death —
He shall be slain, he that so many slay'th,
Yea, by God's dignity, ere it be night !"
    And so all three together made their plight
To live and die each one of them for other,
As though he had been born the other's brother.
And in this drunken passion forth they started,
And toward that very village they departed
Of which the tavern-keeper spoke before.
And then full many a grisly oath they swore,
And rent the Saviour's body limb from limb —
Death should be dead if they discovered him !
When they had travelled hardly half a mile,
Just as they would have stepped across a stile,
They chanced to meet a poor and aged man.
This old man meekly spake, and thus began

To greet them: "May God look upon you, sirs !"
    The greatest braggart of these rioters
Replied: "Now curse thee, churl !   What, where apace ?
Why all wrapped up and hidden save thy face ?
How darest thou live so long in Death's defy ?"
    Straightway this old man looked him in the eye
And answered thus: "Because I cannot meet
A man, by country way or city street,
Though unto Ind I made a pilgrimage,
Willing to give his youth and take my age !
So must I have my age in keeping still,
As long a time, indeed, as God shall will.

    "Nor Death, alas ! will have my life from me;
So like a wretch I wander restlessly
And on the ground, which is my mother's gate,
Knock with my staff and cry both early and late,
'Mother, belovèd Mother, let me in !
See how I wither, flesh and blood and skin;
Alas my bones ! When shall they be at rest ?
Mother, how gladly would I change my chest
That in my room so long a time hath been —
Yea, for a hair-cloth I could wrap me in !'
But yet she will not do me this poor grace:
Wherefore all pale and withered is my face.

    "But, sirs, ye lack in common courtesy
That to an aged man speak villainy
When he hath sinned neither in word nor deed.
For well in holy writings may ye read,
'Before an aged man, whose hair is gray,
Ye should arise'; and therefore thus I say:
To an old man no hurt or evil do,
No more than ye would have men do to you

In your old age, if ye so long abide.
And God be with you, where ye walk or ride —
I must be gone where I have need to go."
    "Nay now, old rogue ! By God, thou shalt not so !"
Answered another rioter anon;
"Thou partest not so lightly, by Saint John !
Thou spake right now of that same traitor Death
That in this country all our comrades slay'th;
Have here my word: thou art a spy of his !
Then take the worst, or tell us where he is,
By God and by the Holy Sacrament !
For truly, thou art of his covenant,
To slay young folk like us, thou false intriguer !"
    "Now, sirs," he answered, "since ye be so eager
To find this Death, turn up that crooked way;
There in yon wood I left him, sooth to say,
Under a tree, and there he will abide.
Not for your boasting will he run and hide.
See ye that oak tree ? Ye shall find him there.
God, that redeemed mankind, save you and spare,
And better you !" Thus spoke this aged man;
And toward the tree these drunken rascals ran
All three, and there, about its roots, they found
Of golden florins, minted fine and round,
Well nigh eight bushels lying, as they thought.
No longer then the traitor Death they sought,
But each was made so happy by the sight
Of all those florins shining fair and bright
That down they sat beside the precious hoard.
The worst of them was first to speak his word.
    "Brothers," he said, "take heed of what I say;
My wit is great, although I jest and play !

Fortune hath found it fit to give this treasure
That we may live our lives in lust and pleasure;
Lightly it comes — so shall it melt away !
God's dignity ! Who would have dreamed today
That we should have so fine and fair a grace ?
But could the gold be carried from this place
Home to my house, or else to one of yours —
For well we know that all this gold is ours —
Then were we in a high felicity !
But such a thing by day could never be;
Men would proclaim us thieves and cause our seizure;
Might even make us hang for our own treasure !
This gold must then be carried hence by night
With secrecy and cautious oversight.
Wherefore I say, draw lot among us all,
And let us mark the way the lot shall fall;
And he that draws it shall with willing heart
And nimble pace toward the town depart,
And fetch in secret wine and bread, and we
That stay behind shall guard full carefully
This gold; and if our comrade does not tarry,
When it is night we will this treasure carry
Wherever by agreement shall be planned."
Then one held out the lots within his hand,
And bade them draw, and look where it would fall;
And it fell on the youngest of them all,
And so by compact toward the town he started.
And scarce a moment after he departed
The one of them spoke slyly to the other:
"Thou know'st well thou art sworn to be my brother;
Now something to thy profit will I say.
Thou see'st our fellow takes himself away;

And here is gold, and that great quantity,
That shall be portioned out among us three.
Nevertheless, if I could shape it so
That we should share it all between us two,
Had I not done a comrade's turn by thee ?"

The other said: "But that could never be !
He knows we two are here and guard the gold;
What could we do ?   What wouldst thou have him told ?"

"Shall what I say be secret ?" asked the first;
"Then shortly shall the method be rehearsed
Whereby I think to bring it well about."
"Agreed," replied the other, "out of doubt
I will betray thee not, as God is true."

"Now," said the first, "thou know'st that we are two,
And two of us are mightier than one.
Watch when he sits, then go as if in fun —
As thou wouldst play about with him, and grip him,
And with my dagger through his sides I'll rip him,
While thou art struggling with him, as in play;
And see thou use thy knife the self-same way.
Then all this treasure shall belong to none,
My dearest friend, but me and thee alone !
Then may we sate our lusts until we tire
And play at dice whenever we desire !"
And thus these rascals have devised a way
To slay the third, as ye have heard me say.

This youngest, he that journeyed to the town,
Within his heart rolled often up and down
The beauty of these florins new and bright.
"O Lord !" quoth he, "If it were so I might
Have all this treasure to myself alone,
There liveth no man underneath the throne

Of God, that might exist more merrily
Than I !" And so the fiend, our enemy,
Put in his head that he should poison buy
Wherewith to make his two companions die;
Because the fiend found him in such a state
That he had leave his fall to consummate,
For it was out of doubt his full intent
To slay them both, and never to repent !
So forth he goes — no longer will he tarry —
Unto a town, to an apothecary,
And prays for poison to exterminate
Some rats, and pole-cats that had robbed of late
His roosts — and he would wreak him, if he might,
On vermin that tormented him by night.
    Then this apothecary, answering:
"God save my soul, but thou shalt have a thing
That, let a living creature drink or eat
No bigger portion than a grain of wheat,
And he shall die, and that in shorter while,
By God, than thou wouldst take to walk a mile —
This poison is so strong and violent."
    All on his cursèd wickedness intent,
This rascal ran as fast as he could fly,
Bearing the poison, to a street near by,
And got three bottles of a man he knew;
And then he poured his poison in the two,
But in the third, his own, put none at all.
For all the night he thought to heave and haul
Carrying gold — then would he slake his thirst.
And so this rascal (may he be accurst !)
Filled all his bottles full of wine; and then
Back to his fellows he repaired again.

What need is there to sermon of it more ?
For just as they had planned his death before,
They slew him now, and quickly.　Then the one
Spoke to the other after it was done:
"Now let us eat and drink and make us merry,
And afterwards we will his body bury."
And so by chance he drank, that very minute,
Out of a bottle with the poison in it,
And gave his comrade drink when he was through,
From which in little while they died, the two.
　　But truly Avicenna, I suppose,
Wrote never in his canons of such throes
And wondrous agonies of poisoning
As these two wretches had in perishing.
Thus died these murderers of whom I tell,
And he who falsely poisoned them as well.

The Book of the Duchess

The Book of the Duchess

My thought was thus — that it was May
And in the dawning there I lay
(This was my dream) in my bed all naked —
And I looked about, for I was wakèd
By little birds, a goodly number,
That had shaken me from out my slumber
With noise and sweetness of their song.
And, so I dreamed, they sat along
My chamber roof outside the whiles,
And sang there, sitting on the tiles,
Warbling each one in his own way,
The sweetest concert, the most gay
That ever men could hear, I trow.
For some sang high and some sang low
Yet all their song made one accord,
To say it shortly, in a word,
Never was there heard so sweet a song
Save one that did to heaven belong;
So merry the sound, so fair each tune is,
I would not for the town of Tunis
But I had heard them as they sang,
For sweetly all my chamber rang
With the singing of their harmony.

159

No instrument or melody
Was ever heard by half so sweet
Nor in its blending half so meet,
For never a bird raised up his voice
In song, but shrewdly made he choice
Finding him strong and merry notes
To sing — they did not spare their throats.
And, truth to say, my chamber was
Made fair with paintings, and with glass
Its windows well were glazed and clear,
And never a hole or crack was there,
That to behold it was great joy.
And wholly there the tale of Troy
Was in the glazing fashioned thus;
Of Hector and King Priamus,
Of Achilles and of Lamedon;
Of Queen Medea and Jasòn,
Paris and Helen and Lavyne.
And all the walls with colors fine
Were painted, showing, text and gloze,
All of The Romance of the Rose.
Closed were my windows every one,
And through the bright glass shone the sun
And scattered on my bed his beams
That fell in glad and gilded streams;
And the sky too was very fair;
Blue, bright, and clear was all the air —
Tempered, in truth, all mild and sweet;
For neither cold there was nor heat,
Nor in the broad sky any cloud.
And as I lay thus, wondrous loud
Meseemed I heard a hunter blow

His horn, as trying it out to know
If it were clear or hoarse of sound.
And trampling heard I, all around,
Of hounds and horses and of men;
And much talk was of hunting then:
How they had gone to slay the hart,
How he had won at length apart
To covert, and I know not what.
But all at once, on hearing that —
How they would hunt, right glad was I,
And I was up; full speedily
Left I the chamber and took my horse;
So forth, and never stayed my course
Until I reached the field without.
And there I found a mighty rout —
Huntsmen, and many foresters
With hounds in relay, and lymeres;
These to the forest hied them fast,
And I along, and so at last
I asked one leading a lymere:
"Say, fellow, who goes hunting here ?"
Quoth I; the forester said thus:
"Sir, 'tis th'Emperor Octavius,
He hunts; and rideth here near by."
"By God's grace, in good time," said I,
"Faster !" and so began to ride.
And when we reached the forest-side
Each one, according to his wont,
Forthwith prepared himself to hunt.
The Master of the Hunt blew three
Notes on a great horn lustily
At the uncoupling of the hounds,

And soon they stir the hart, that bounds
Away, hallooed and followed fast
For a long time; but then at last
This hart by ruse hath stolen away
From all the hounds a secret way.
The hounds all ran beyond his trail
And nosed about to no avail
Until the huntsman blew a blast
And sounded the recall at last.
 Now I was walking from my tree,
And as I went, there came to me
A whelp, that fawned me as I stood —
It had followed, but could do no good.
It came toward me just as though
It knew me — crept along so low,
Held down its head and joined its ears
And laid back smoothly all its hairs.
I reached for it; but suddenly
It fled, and so was gone from me;
And after it I seemed to stray
Along a green and flowery way,
Full thick with grass, full soft and sweet,
Sown all with flowers fair under feet,
And little used: or it seemed thus;
For Flora both and Zephyrus,
Those two that bless the growing flowers,
Here, I believe, had built their bowers.
Yea, one to look thereon had thought
That here the earth, with envy wrought,
Made strife to be more gay than heaven —
More flowers to have, all like the seven
Stars that in the welkin be.

It had forgotten the poverty
That winter with his frosty morrows
Had made it suffer, and all its sorrows —
All was forgotten — 'twas plain to see,
For green grew every woodland tree —
Sweetness of dew had made them grow.

   Nor is it need ye ask to know
If here were green groves, or if these
Were thick with trunks of full-leafed trees;
And every tree stood by himself,
Well ten feet from the next, or twelve.
Such mighty trees, of such great strength,
Of forty or fifty fathom's length
Clean up without a bough or stick,
With tops so broad of spread, so thick,
(Never an inch were they asunder)
That it was always shadow under
Their roof.   And many a hart and hind
Was both before me and behind;
Of fawns and sorrels, bucks and does,
Was the wood full, and many roes;
And many squirrels too, that sate
Full high upon the trees, and ate,
And in their fashion made their feasts.
In short, it was so full of beasts
That even if Argus the noble counter
Should set to reckon upon his counter
Reckoning with his figures ten
For by those figures all may ken —
If they be wise, and reckon and number
And tell of everything the number —

Still should he fail to count aright
The wonders that I dreamed that night.
   But forth they wandered wondrous fast
Down through the wood, and so at last
I was aware of a man in black
That sat before me, with his back
Leaning against a huge oak tree.
And "Lord !" I thought, "Who may that be ?
What ails him to be sitting here ?"
So thinking, straightway I drew near;
Then found I lying by the tree
A knight of wondrous courtesy —
Or by his manner he seemed so —
And great of wealth, and young thereto;
Of four and twenty years appeared
His age, and scanty was his beard;
He was apparelled all in black.
I walked up close behind his back
And there I stood as still as aught,
So that, in truth, he saw me not,
His head being bowed toward the ground.
And with a deathly, sorrowful sound
He made ten lines of rhyme or so,
A love complaint, singing it low,
The saddest, the most piteous
I ever heard, and I say thus:
It was great wonder that kind nature
Could suffer any living creature
To have such sorrow and not be dead.
With cheek all drained of any red
A kind of song I heard him croon
Without a lilt, without a tune,

And it was this, for well I can
Remember it: thus it began:

> Sorrow have I in such degree
> There is no room for joy in me,
> Now that I see my lady bright,
> She whom I loved with my full might
> Gone forth from me, and utterly.
>
> Alas, O Death, what aileth thee
> That thou shouldst not have taken me
> When thou didst take my lady fair
> That was so bright, so fresh, so free,
> So good, that nowhere men could see
> Goodness that might with hers compare.

When he had made thus his complaint,
At once his woeful heart grew faint,
Suddenly went his spirits dead,
His very blood ebbed back in dread
Down to his heart to make it warm;
For well it felt the heart had harm.
    But at the end he saw I stood
Before him and had doffed my hood
And greeted him as best I could,
Graciously, and not too loud.
He said, "I pray thee, be not wroth;
"I heard thee not, to say full truth;
Nor did I see thee, certainly."
"Good sir, no matter !" answered I.
"I am right sorry if I have aught
Disturbed or troubled you from your thought;
Forgive, I pray you, my mistake."
"Surely !   The amend is light to make,"

He answered me, "for there is none !
Nothing there is missaid or done."
"Sir," said I then, "the hunt is over;
This hart, I hold, hath got him cover;
They will not find him anywhere."
"Nothing," he said, "for that I care.
I give no thought at all thereto."
"Now by our Lord, I think it true.
Your look proves well the word ye say.
Yet one thing let me ask you, pray.
Meseemeth in great sorrow ye be;
But if ye would reveal to me
Some portion, truly, of your woe,
As sure as God shall help me, so
If I could mend you — that would I.
This may ye prove will ye but try.
Tell me your sorrow:.perchance the smart
Will stop thereby and ease your. heart
That seems full sick beneath your side."
At that he looked at me aside
As if to say: "That never will be !"
"The best of thanks, good friend," said he.
"I thank thee that thou wouldst it so;
And yet thou canst not do it.   No,
None liveth that can this sorrow lighten
That maketh cheek to fall and whiten,
And leaveth heart and wit forlorn
Till me is woe that I was born !

   "My boldness is all turned to shame;
Fortune the false hath played a game
Of chess with me, alas ! the while !

That traitress false and full of guile.
She is false, and ever laughing
With one eye, with the other weeping.
What is aloft, that pulls she down.
I liken her to the scorpion
That false and flattering is, for while
With head he maketh praise and smile,
All midways in his flattering
He casts his sharp tail out to sting
And poison you; and so will she.
She is an envious charity
That ever is false, though it look well;
So turneth she her fickle wheel
About, and it is nowise stable,
But now by the fire, now by the table;
Full many a one she blinds this way.
Like an enchantment doth she play,
That seemeth one, yet is not so.
The false, false thief !   But dost thou know
What she hath done ?   Hark while I say:
At chess with me she came to play,
And by false moves, ere I had seen,
She stole on me and took my queen.
And when I saw my queen was gone,
Alas !   I could not then play on,
But said, 'Farewell, my sweet, to thee,
And farewell all that ever shall be !'
Then forthwith, 'Check, here !' Fortune cried,
And 'Mate !' and on the board did slide
A fatal, wandering pawn, alas !
For craftier at play she was
Than Attalus, that made a game

First out of chess — such was his name.
    But through that queen am I forlorn
Of bliss ! And ! that I was born !
I have more sorrow than Tantalus."
    And when I heard this piteous
Tale of his, told as I have said,
Scarce could I longer stay — so bled
My heart for him with a great woe.
"Ah, good sir !" cried I, "say not so !
Think you on Socrates, who never
Would care three straws for whatsoever
Fortune had will or power to do."
"No," said he, then. "I cannot so."
"For God's sake, why, good sir ?" quoth I,
"Do not say this, for certainly
Though ye had lost twelve queens, and so
Should slay yourself in grief and woe,
Ye should be damned in such a pass
As justly as Medea was
That slew her children for Jasòn;
And Phyllis, too, for Demophon
That hanged herself, ah ! welaway !
Because he broke the appointed day
For meeting her. Another rage
Had Dido, too, Queen of Carthàge,
That slew herself for the falsity
Æneas did — what fool was she !
And Echo died because Narcissus
Refused his love; and like to this is
Many another folly done.
And for Delilah died Samson,
That with a pillar wrought his death.

But no man is there drawing breath
That for a queen would make such woe !"
"Why not ?" quoth he; "It is not so.
Thy words are deeper than they seem;
I have lost more than thou dost dream."
"Lo, sir, how may that be ?" quoth I.
"Good sir, tell me in full the why,
And in what wise, how, and wherefore
Ye have lost the bliss ye had before."
"Freely.   Come hither and be seated,
And all the tale shall be repeated
If only thou in every way
Give heed, and hearken what I say.

   "Unto a certain place one day
I came, and saw a great array
Of ladies — the fairest company
That ever any man did see
At once assembled.   Shall I say
Chance only made me go that way ?
Nay, but the cursèd trickery
Of Fortune, she that loves to lie —
She the false traitress, the perverse:
Would God that I could call her worse,
Who worketh me the deepest woe;
Soon will I tell why this is so.

   "I looked upon those ladies there,
And was in little time aware
How one shone bright from all the rout.
For I dare swear beyond a doubt
That as the summer sun is bright
And fair and clear and full of light
Beyond all planets in the heaven,

Or moon, or star of all the seven
For all the world — even so had she
Above these others sovereignty
In beauty, manner, and comeliness,
In stature and proper gladsomeness,
In goodness all men praise so well —
In short, what more is there to tell ?
For every hair upon her head,
To speak the truth, it was not red,
Nor yellow it appeared to me,
Nor brown, but gold it seemed to be !
And what an eye my lady had !
For it was gay, good, glad and sad,
Modest, well-shaped, and not too wide,
And never slyly looked aside,
Nor overboldly, but it shone
So fair, it drew in everyone
That gazed on her.   And her eyes seemed
As if — or so at least fools dreamed —
They would have mercy, but always this
Was in the testing proved amiss.
That glance was born of no false ways,
But it was all her own pure gaze.
For Goddess Nature fashioned those
Her eyes to open and to close
Gently; they would not spread them wide
Whatever joy there might betide;
Nor wildly, even in merriest play,
But ever, methought, they seemed to say:
'My wrath is gone and I forgive.'
Therewith she loved so well to live
That dullness was of her adread.

Neither too sober nor too glad
She was; but rather always bore
Herself with measure — none had more.
 "And what a face she had thereto !
Alas ! my heart sinks down with woe
For lack of English and of wit
Enough to let me tell of it,
Setting its beauty out in full.
Also my spirit hath grown too dull
For such great task to make device.
I have no wit that could suffice
To know the thing her beauty is,
Yet will I say as much as this:
That she was fresh and ruddy-hued,
And every day her beauty newed.
 "So smooth and comely was her neck
There was no sign of bone or break
Upon its whiteness that missat,
And it was straight and smooth and flat
Without a. hollow, and collar-bone
By her appearance, had she none.
Her throat, as I have memory,
Seemed a round tower of ivory,
Good-sized, and yet not more than right.
They called my lady good, fair WHITE,
And fitting was that name for her,
For bright she was and also fair;
Truly her name was nowise wrong.
Shoulders right fair she had, and long
Her body was.   Her arms were light
And yet well-fleshed; her hands were white
And the nails red, and round each breast,

And broad the hips to give good rest
Unto the straightness of her back.
I knew in her no other lack,
For all things in proportion were
That I could know by sight of her.

"And thereto could she be so gay
At pleasure, I will dare to say
That she was like a torch, so bright
That every man may take its light,
And yet it never shines the less.

"In manner and in comeliness
So went it with any lady dear;
For man or woman of her cheer
Might have his fill had he but sight
To see her loveliness aright.
For I will swear that even among
Ten thousand others in a throng
She would have been of one and all
Chief mirror of the festival,
Though they should range them in a row
For every eye to see and know.
And whether at feast or revelry
As empty seemed the company
Without her, as a golden crown
With all its shining jewels gone.
Truly she seemed unto my eye
The phœnix bird of Araby
Of which there liveth never but one —
For such as she was, knew I none.

"Right on this same, as I have said,
All love in me was wholly laid;
In that sweet lady my content,

My joy, my very life were blent,
So was I hers, — yea, all and wholly."
"By our Lord, I do believe you fully !
Sure, ye did right to love this way;
Better ye might not do, I say."
"Better ! Nay, none so well !" quoth he.
"Sir, I believe it, certainly !"
"Believe it well." "Sir, so I do !"
"I do believe that this is true:
It seemed to you she was the rarest
Of ladies, of all fair the fairest
To any that saw her with your sight !"
"With mine ! Nay there was none that might
See her, but swore that it was so.
Yet would I love her best, even though
They had not, even did I possess
The beauty of Alcibiades,
And all the strength of Hercules
And thereto had the worthiness
Of Alexander, and all richesse
That ever was in Babylon,
In Carthage or in Macedon.
   "To keep myself from idleness
I made, in truth, a business
Of shaping songs as best I could,
And these I often sang aloud
And worked upon them a great deal,
Though never made I songs so well
Nor understood the art withal
Fully, like Lamech's son Tubal
That first found out the art of song,
Hearing the hammers beating strong

Upon the anvil, high and low;
From this he made his first songs grow.
But the Greeks say Pythagoras
Discoverer and finder was
Of song; Aurora telleth so —
But they are nothing here, these two.
At any rate, these songs I made
To tell my feeling, and make glad
My heart, and lo !   This was the first;
I know not whether it was the worst:

Lord, my heart grows lightlier
Thinking upon the sweet of her
That is so seemly for to see;
I wish to God that it could be
That she would hold me for her knight,
My lady all so fair and bright!

Now have I told thee, sooth to say,
My first song.   And it chanced one day
I fixed my mind upon the woe
I suffered, and the sorrow slow
For her, and yet she knew it naught.
I did not dare to tell my thought.
'Alas, I have no way,' I said.
'Unless I tell her, I am but dead,
And if I tell her, certainly
I fear that she will angry be.
What shall I do?'
                    "In this debate
My strife and sorrow grew so great
I thought my heart must burst in two.

But at the end of all this woe
I did bethink myself that nature
Had never dowered any creature
With beauty and with goodness so,
Without the gift of mercy too.
And so it happened, when my heart
Had come again, I made a start
And, to tell briefly all my speech,
With my whole heart did I beseech
That she would be my lady, and swore
And promised her forevermore
Steadfast in all to be, and true,
And fresh to keep my love and new,
And never another lady serve,
But her own worship to preserve
As best I could.   I swore her this:
'Yours shall be all there ever is
Forevermore, my heart's own sweet !
And I will do you no deceit,
Unless I dream.   God keep me true !'
And when at last my tale was through,
God knows I thought she did not care
A straw for all I told her there.
To tell it shortly as she said it
In truth, her answer thus she made it:
I cannot give it word for word,
But the whole sum of what I heard
Of her reply — she answered 'Nay'
All finally.   Alas ! that day
Of grief I suffered and of woe !
That even Cassandra, she that so
Bewailed destruction that was come

To Troy-town and to Ilium,
Had never the grief that then I knew.
But nothing dared I say thereto
For outright fear.   I stole away
And thus I lived full many a day,
And in those days I had no need
To stir, in truth, beyond my bed
Seeking for sorrow; each morning he
Stood at my side in wait for me,
My love was so unchangeable.
    "So with another year it fell
That once again I thought to show
(That she might understand and know)
My sorrow.   And she understood
That I had willed for naught but good,
And honor, and to keep her name
Above all others, and free from shame,
And served her all so eagerly
That it was pity I should die,
Since that I meant no thing amiss;
So when my lady knew all this
My lady gave me utterly
The noble gift of her mercy,
And unto me a ring she gave —
The first thing ever I did have
Of her.   No need is there to say
Whether my heart grew glad that day !
So help me God, I was as glad
As though from death to life I had
Been raised — of all haps this was best,
The gladdest and most full of rest.
And that sweet lady, my delight,

When I had wrong and she had right,
Always in her great goodness she
Would grant forgiveness graciously.
With all my youth, for every chance
She took me under governance.
   "Therewith she always lived so true
Our joy was ever fresh and new;
Our two hearts were so much a pair
That never any woe was there
That thrust itself between the two;
For always, of a truth, they knew
One bliss, one sorrow for the both,
Together glad, together wroth:
All things for us were of one cheer.
And thus we lived full many a year
So well, I cannot tell you how."
"Sir," quoth I then, "Where is she now?"
"Now!" he exclaimed, and with a groan
He turned as dead as any stone,
And said, "Alas, that I should be!
That was the loss I told to thee —
The heavy loss I said I bore.
Bethink thee how I said before:
'Thy words are deeper than they seem;
I have lost more than thou dost dream.'
Alas, God knows that it was she!"
"Alas, sir! What! How can that be?"
"She is dead." "Nay." "Yes, by my name!"
"Is that your loss? God, what a shame!"
Scarce had I spoke, when one by one
The crowd streamed back, and all was done
For that time, with the hart-hunting.

With that, it seeemd to me, this king
Quickly for home began to ride —
Unto a place that stood beside
The wood, but little space away —
A castle, long, white-walled, that lay,
On a high hill, above a dell.
So did I dream; thus it befell.

The Golden Age

A BLISSFUL life, a peaceable and sweet,
  In the golden age the happy peoples led,
They were content with fruits they found to eat,
  Which in the fields about they gatherèd,
With no excesses were they surfeited;
  Unknown were both the hand and water mill;
On nuts and haws and other mast they fed,
  And deep of cold spring water drank their fill.

The earth was not yet wounded with the plough,
  Yet corn, unsown of men, sprang all around,
Which they would eat, with fruits from many a bough;
  No man had sent a furrow through his ground,
No man in flint the hidden fire had found,
  Untilled and all untended lay the vine,
No mortars were there then, no spice to pound
  For clarey or for sauce of galantine.

No dyer with his weld or woad was there,
  But every fleece was of its natural hue,
No flesh knew violence of edge or spear,
  Men knew no coin, to call it false or true;
No ship had ploughed the waves of green and blue,

No merchants homeward fetched their foreign ware,
No trumpet's call to war the people knew,
    No soaring towers, no ramparts round or square.

Of what avail were battle in that day?
    No profit was, no wealth for which to fight,
But cursed was the evil time, I say,
    When sweating men began to dig to light
Metals deep-lurking in the earthy night,
    And first knew gems, and in the rivers sought them,
Alas ! then sprang to life the cursèd blight
    Of avarice, and their first sorrow brought them.

Tyrants press not to sniff the battle breeze
    With only brush or wilderness to win
Where all is poor — as saith Diogenes —
    Where victual likewise is so scarce and thin
That only apples grow, and nuts therein;
    But after wine and food in wealthy vault,
And bags of gold they go, and shun no sin
    With all their host the city to assault.

Then were no palace chambers, then no halls;
    In caverns and in forests soft and sweet,
The blessèd people slumbered free of walls,
    On grass and leaves in quietness complete;
No feathered down, no bleachèd linen sheet
    Was known to them, yet all secure they slept,
Their hearts unstirred by dreams of envious brawls;
    For each of them his faith with other kept.

Unforged was hauberk then or armor-plate;
 The lamblike folk, of vices wholly free,
Had yet no fantasy for strife or hate,
 But each the other cherished lovingly;
No envy, avarice, or tyranny
 With heavy toll, no lord they knew, no pride,
But humbleness and peace had empery,
 And good faith shared the kingship by their side.

Not yet had Jupiter the gluttonous —
 Who fathered first the lust for luxury —
Appeared, nor Nimrod, all desirous
 To reign, and raise his monstrous towers on high;
Alas ! alas ! now men may weep and cry,
 Treason and greed are rulers in these days,
Envy and poison and duplicity
 And shameful murder done in devious ways.

Rosemound

MADAME, all beauty maketh you its shrine
As far as goes the map of earthly ground;
For like a crystal gloriously ye shine;
Like rubies glow your cheeks so red and round.
Also so merrily ye trip around,
That at a revel when I see you dance
It is an ointment laid upon my wound,
Though ye with me will do no dalliance.

For though I weep of tears a cask of brine
Yet all that woe may not my heart confound;
Your lovely voice ye send so small and fine
Foldeth my thought with joy and bliss around;
I go in love so exquisitely bound
I murmur in a penitential trance,
"Enough for me to love you, Rosemound,
Though ye with me will do no dalliance !"

No pike was ever steeped in galantine
As I in love am wrapped about and wound,
And hence I often of myself divine
A second Tristram may in me be found !

This love of mine may not be cooled or drowned,
Ever I burn in amorous pleasánce:
Do what ye please, I will your thrall be found,
Though ye with me will do no dalliance !

Alceste is Here

HIDE, Absalom, thy golden tresses clear,
Esther, lay down thy meekness utterly;
Conceal, O Jonathan, thy friendly cheer,
And Marcia Cato and Penelope,
Bring not your wifehood here for rivalry;
Hide all your beauties, Iseult and Elaine:
Alceste is here, all else is dull and vain !

Let not thy form, Lavinia, appear,
Nor thou, Lucrece, nor sad Polixine
That for thy love wast doomed to pay so dear;
And Cleopatra, let thine honesty,
Thy passion, thy renown, all hidden be;
Thisbe, show not thine ecstasy and pain:
Alceste is here, all else is dull and vain !

Laodamia, Hero, come not here
With Dido; Phyllis, hanged so wretchedly
For Demophon, and thou of heavy cheer
O Canacé, and thou, Hypsipyle,
Betrayed by Jason, make no boastful cry;
Nor dare thou, Ariadne, to complain:
Alceste is here, all else is dull and vain !

Now Welcome, Summer

Now welcome, summer, with thy sunlight soft,
That all the winter weather put to flight
And scattered from the earth the long black night !

Saint Valentine, that sittest high aloft,
For thee the birds are singing their delight:
Now welcome, summer, with thy sunlight soft,
That all the winter weather put to flight !

Well may they sing to thee, rejoicing oft,
For each of them hath found his mate aright,
And wakes and sings his joy with all his might:
Now welcome, summer, with thy sunlight soft,
That all the winter weather put to flight,
And scattered from the earth the long black night !

The Complaint of Chaucer to His Empty Purse

To you, my purse, and to no other wight,
Complain I — for you are my lady dear;
I am so sorry now that ye are light —
For truly, unless ye make me heavy cheer
I had as lief be laid upon my bier;
Wherefore unto your mercy thus I cry:
Be heavy for me again or else I die!

Vouchsafe me, purse, this day — ere it be night —
That I from you the blissful sound may hear —
Or see your color like the sun's own light,
Whose yellowness has never had a peer!
Ye are my life, the star by which I steer,
The queen of comfort and good company:
Be heavy for me again or else I die!

Now purse, my worldly saviour, my life's light,
If ye'll not be my banker, as I fear,
At least deliver me by your sovereign might
Out of this town, for I am shaved as near

As any friar; and yet, since ye are here,
Once more I pray unto your courtesy:
Be heavy for me again or else I die !

ENVOY [TO KING HENRY IV]

O CONQUEROR of Brutus' Albion,
Whom now free vote and royal blood have won
True kingship: unto you this song I send;
And ye, that all misfortune can amend,
Give mind to what I pray, and have it done !

Truth

FLEE from the crowd and dwell with Truth.   The fate
Thou hast — accept it, though it be but small,
For mobs are envious, hoarding breedeth hate,
Good fortune blinds, and he who climbs may fall.
Taste what behooves thee, clamor not for all,
Act well thyself ere thou adviser be,
And doubt it not: the Truth shall make thee free.

Be not in storm to set the crooked straight,
Trusting in her that turneth like a ball;
The peace that lies in little things is great;
Turn not to discontent in general;
Strive not as strove the pitcher with the wall;
Subdue thyself with thy severity
And doubt it not: the Truth shall make thee free.

That which is sent, with cheerfulness await:
The wrestling for this world invites a fall;
Here is no home, but waste-land desolate —
Forth, pilgrim, forth !   Forth, beast, out of thy stall !
Know thine own land, look up, thank God for all,
Hold the highroad, thy spirit guiding thee,
And doubt it not: the Truth shall make thee free.

Therefore, thou beast, leave thine old beast's estate
Unto the world; cease now to be a thrall;
Ask mercy of thy God that did create
Thy soul from nothing; draw to Him and call
In prayer on Him for others, one and all,
And for thyself, His heavenly clemency;
And doubt it not: the Truth shall make thee free.

NOTE

The meaning of the following words may be noted:

prime — 9 A. M.

lectuaries — remedies

lymere — a dog in leash

steven — voice

vernicle — a copy **of** the sacred handkerchief on which could be seen the imprint of the Saviour's face.

With regard to "The Book of the Duchess," the reader should remember that this poem was written on the occasion of the death of Blanche, wife of John of Gaunt, Duke of Lancaster, fourth son of King Edward III of England. In a line on page 171 — "They called my lady good fair WHITE," Chaucer refers specifically to the duchess by using the English equivalent of her name.

2 171

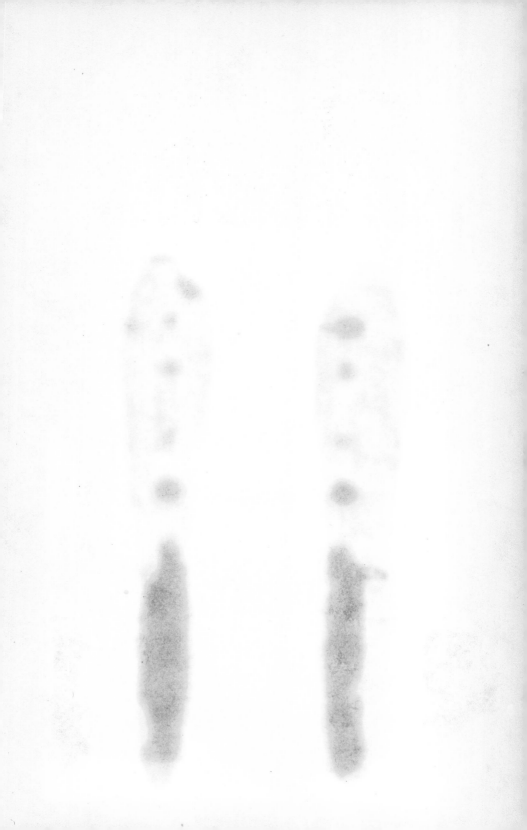

10212

CHAUCER, GEOFFREY
    THE CANTERBURY TALES.

PR
1870
A1
H8